Chief Investment Officer
Complete Self-Assessment C

The guidance in this Self-Assessment
Officer best practices and standards i
design and quality management. The .... is also based on the
professional judgment of the individual collaborators listed in the
Acknowledgments.

Notice of rights

**You are licensed to use the Self-Assessment contents in your
presentations and materials for internal use and customers
without asking us - we are here to help.**

All rights reserved for the book itself: this book may not be reproduced
or transmitted in any form by any means, electronic, mechanical,
photocopying, recording, or otherwise, without the prior written
permission of the publisher.

The information in this book is distributed on an "As Is" basis without
warranty. While every precaution has been taken in the preparation of he
book, neither the author nor the publisher shall have any liability to any
person or entity with respect to any loss or damage caused or alleged to
be caused directly or indirectly by the instructions contained in this book
or by the products described in it.

Trademarks

Many of the designations used by manufacturers and sellers to
distinguish their products are claimed as trademarks. Where those
designations appear in this book, and the publisher was aware of a
trademark claim, the designations appear as requested by the owner
of the trademark. All other product names and services identified
throughout this book are used in editorial fashion only and for the
benefit of such companies with no intention of infringement of the
trademark. No such use, or the use of any trade name, is intended to
convey endorsement or other affiliation with this book.

Copyright © by The Art of Service
http://theartofservice.com
service@theartofservice.com

Table of Contents

About The Art of Service

The Art of Service, Business Process Architects since 2000, is dedicated to helping stakeholders achieve excellence.

Defining, designing, creating, and implementing a process to solve a stakeholders challenge or meet an objective is the most valuable role... In EVERY group, company, organization and department.

Unless you're talking a one-time, single-use project, there should be a process. Whether that process is managed and implemented by humans, AI, or a combination of the two, it needs to be designed by someone with a complex enough perspective to ask the right questions.

Someone capable of asking the right questions and step back and say, 'What are we really trying to accomplish here? And is there a different way to look at it?'

With The Art of Service's Standard Requirements Self-Assessments, we empower people who can do just that — whether their title is marketer, entrepreneur, manager, salesperson, consultant, Business Process Manager, executive assistant, IT Manager, CIO etc... —they are the people who rule the future. They are people who watch the process as it happens, and ask the right questions to make the process work better.

Contact us when you need any support with this Self-Assessment and any help with templates, blue-prints and examples of standard documents you might need:

http://theartofservice.com
service@theartofservice.com

Included Resources - how to access

Included with your purchase of the book is the Chief Investment

Officer Self-Assessment Spreadsheet Dashboard which contains all questions and Self-Assessment areas and auto-generates insights, graphs, and project RACI planning - all with examples to get you started right away.

How? Simply send an email to
access@theartofservice.com
with this books' title in the subject to get the Chief Investment Officer Self Assessment Tool right away.

You will receive the following contents with New and Updated specific criteria:

• The latest quick edition of the book in PDF

• The latest complete edition of the book in PDF, which criteria correspond to the criteria in...

• The Self-Assessment Excel Dashboard, and...

• Example pre-filled Self-Assessment Excel Dashboard to get familiar with results generation

• In-depth specific Checklists covering the topic

• Project management checklists and templates to assist with implementation

INCLUDES LIFETIME SELF ASSESSMENT UPDATES

Every self assessment comes with Lifetime Updates and Lifetime Free Updated Books. Lifetime Updates is an industry-first feature which allows you to receive verified self assessment updates, ensuring you always have the most accurate information at your fingertips.

Get it now- you will be glad you did - do it now, before you forget.

Send an email to **access@theartofservice.com** with this books' title in the subject to get the Chief Investment Officer Self Assessment Tool right away.

Purpose of this Self-Assessment

This Self-Assessment has been developed to improve understanding of the requirements and elements of Chief Investment Officer, based on best practices and standards in business process architecture, design and quality management.

It is designed to allow for a rapid Self-Assessment to determine how closely existing management practices and procedures correspond to the elements of the Self-Assessment.

The criteria of requirements and elements of Chief Investment Officer have been rephrased in the format of a Self-Assessment questionnaire, with a seven-criterion scoring system, as explained in this document.

In this format, even with limited background knowledge of Chief Investment Officer, a manager can quickly review existing operations to determine how they measure up to the standards. This in turn can serve as the starting point of a 'gap analysis' to identify management tools or system elements that might usefully be implemented in the organization to help improve overall performance.

How to use the Self-Assessment

On the following pages are a series of questions to identify to what extent your Chief Investment Officer initiative is complete in comparison to the requirements set in standards.

To facilitate answering the questions, there is a space in front of each question to enter a score on a scale of '1' to '5'.

1 Strongly Disagree

2 Disagree

3 Neutral

4 Agree

5 Strongly Agree

Read the question and rate it with the following in front of mind:

'In my belief, the answer to this question is clearly defined'.

There are two ways in which you can choose to interpret this statement;
1. how aware are you that the answer to the question is clearly defined
2. for more in-depth analysis you can choose to gather evidence and confirm the answer to the question. This obviously will take more time, most Self-Assessment users opt for the first way to interpret the question and dig deeper later on based on the outcome of the overall Self-Assessment.

A score of '1' would mean that the answer is not clear at all, where a '5' would mean the answer is crystal clear and defined. Leave emtpy when the question is not applicable or you don't want to answer it, you can skip it without affecting your score. Write your score in the space provided.

After you have responded to all the appropriate statements in each section, compute your average score for that section, using the formula provided, and round to the nearest tenth. Then transfer to the corresponding spoke in the Chief Investment Officer Scorecard on the second next page of the Self-Assessment.

Your completed Chief Investment Officer Scorecard will give you a clear presentation of which Chief Investment Officer areas need attention.

Chief Investment Officer Scorecard Example

Example of how the finalized Scorecard can look like:

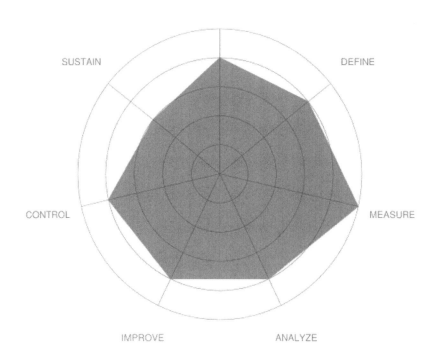

Chief Investment Officer Scorecard

Your Scores:

BEGINNING OF THE SELF-ASSESSMENT:

CRITERION #1: RECOGNIZE

INTENT: Be aware of the need for change. Recognize that there is an unfavorable variation, problem or symptom.

In my belief, the answer to this question is clearly defined:

5 Strongly Agree

4 Agree

3 Neutral

2 Disagree

1 Strongly Disagree

1. What resources or support might you need?
<--- Score

2. What is the problem or issue?
<--- Score

3. Who needs what information?
<--- Score

4. Is the need for organizational change recognized?
<--- Score

5. What do you need to start doing?
<--- Score

6. Where is training needed?
<--- Score

7. What are the clients issues and concerns?
<--- Score

8. How much are sponsors, customers, partners, stakeholders involved in Chief investment officer? In other words, what are the risks, if Chief investment officer does not deliver successfully?
<--- Score

9. How are training requirements identified?
<--- Score

10. Is it needed?
<--- Score

11. What are your needs in relation to Chief investment officer skills, labor, equipment, and markets?
<--- Score

12. What extra resources will you need?
<--- Score

13. How do you recognize an Chief investment officer objection?
<--- Score

14. How can auditing be a preventative security measure?
<--- Score

15. What problems are you facing and how do you consider Chief investment officer will circumvent those obstacles?
<--- Score

16. Did you miss any major Chief investment officer issues?
<--- Score

17. Do you recognize Chief investment officer achievements?
<--- Score

18. Is the quality assurance team identified?
<--- Score

19. What activities does the governance board need to consider?
<--- Score

20. Are there any specific expectations or concerns about the Chief investment officer team, Chief investment officer itself?
<--- Score

21. To what extent would your organization benefit from being recognized as a award recipient?
<--- Score

22. Which issues are too important to ignore?
<--- Score

23. Who should resolve the Chief investment officer issues?
<--- Score

24. What would happen if Chief investment officer weren't done?
<--- Score

25. What vendors make products that address the Chief investment officer needs?
<--- Score

26. Where do you need to exercise leadership?
<--- Score

27. Do you need to avoid or amend any Chief investment officer activities?
<--- Score

28. What are the expected benefits of Chief investment officer to the stakeholder?
<--- Score

29. What is the smallest subset of the problem you can usefully solve?
<--- Score

30. What are the stakeholder objectives to be achieved with Chief investment officer?
<--- Score

31. How do you identify the kinds of information that you will need?
<--- Score

32. What situation(s) led to this Chief investment

officer Self Assessment?
<--- Score

33. Have you identified your Chief investment officer key performance indicators?
<--- Score

34. Do you have/need 24-hour access to key personnel?
<--- Score

35. Who are your key stakeholders who need to sign off?
<--- Score

36. What Chief investment officer problem should be solved?
<--- Score

37. What creative shifts do you need to take?
<--- Score

38. Are you dealing with any of the same issues today as yesterday? What can you do about this?
<--- Score

39. Are there Chief investment officer problems defined?
<--- Score

40. Who needs budgets?
<--- Score

41. How does it fit into your organizational needs and tasks?
<--- Score

42. Is it clear when you think of the day ahead of you what activities and tasks you need to complete?
<--- Score

43. Will new equipment/products be required to facilitate Chief investment officer delivery, for example is new software needed?
<--- Score

44. When a Chief investment officer manager recognizes a problem, what options are available?
<--- Score

45. As a sponsor, customer or management, how important is it to meet goals, objectives?
<--- Score

46. What are the minority interests and what amount of minority interests can be recognized?
<--- Score

47. Are problem definition and motivation clearly presented?
<--- Score

48. Why is this needed?
<--- Score

49. How many trainings, in total, are needed?
<--- Score

50. What is the extent or complexity of the Chief investment officer problem?
<--- Score

51. Are there any revenue recognition issues?
<--- Score

52. How are you going to measure success?
<--- Score

53. How are the Chief investment officer's objectives aligned to the group's overall stakeholder strategy?
<--- Score

54. What needs to stay?
<--- Score

55. Are your goals realistic? Do you need to redefine your problem? Perhaps the problem has changed or maybe you have reached your goal and need to set a new one?
<--- Score

56. Are controls defined to recognize and contain problems?
<--- Score

57. Are employees recognized for desired behaviors?
<--- Score

58. What is the problem and/or vulnerability?
<--- Score

59. Will Chief investment officer deliverables need to be tested and, if so, by whom?
<--- Score

60. Who needs to know about Chief investment officer?
<--- Score

61. Are there regulatory / compliance issues?
<--- Score

62. Consider your own Chief investment officer project, what types of organizational problems do you think might be causing or affecting your problem, based on the work done so far?
<--- Score

63. What Chief investment officer capabilities do you need?
<--- Score

64. Does the problem have ethical dimensions?
<--- Score

65. What else needs to be measured?
<--- Score

66. What training and capacity building actions are needed to implement proposed reforms?
<--- Score

67. Who else hopes to benefit from it?
<--- Score

68. What prevents you from making the changes you know will make you a more effective Chief investment officer leader?
<--- Score

69. For your Chief investment officer project, identify and describe the business environment, is there more than one layer to the business environment?
<--- Score

70. Which needs are not included or involved?
<--- Score

71. What Chief investment officer coordination do you need?
<--- Score

72. Which information does the Chief investment officer business case need to include?
<--- Score

73. Whom do you really need or want to serve?
<--- Score

74. What Chief investment officer events should you attend?
<--- Score

75. What does Chief investment officer success mean to the stakeholders?
<--- Score

76. To what extent does each concerned units management team recognize Chief investment officer as an effective investment?
<--- Score

77. What is the recognized need?
<--- Score

78. Do you need different information or graphics?
<--- Score

79. What are the timeframes required to resolve each of the issues/problems?

<--- Score

80. Can management personnel recognize the monetary benefit of Chief investment officer?
<--- Score

81. What are the Chief investment officer resources needed?
<--- Score

82. What should be considered when identifying available resources, constraints, and deadlines?
<--- Score

83. Would you recognize a threat from the inside?
<--- Score

84. Who needs to know?
<--- Score

85. Do you know what you need to know about Chief investment officer?
<--- Score

86. Are employees recognized or rewarded for performance that demonstrates the highest levels of integrity?
<--- Score

87. Are losses recognized in a timely manner?
<--- Score

88. How do you recognize an objection?
<--- Score

89. What do employees need in the short term?

<--- Score

90. Does your organization need more Chief investment officer education?
<--- Score

91. What information do users need?
<--- Score

92. Does Chief investment officer create potential expectations in other areas that need to be recognized and considered?
<--- Score

93. How do you assess your Chief investment officer workforce capability and capacity needs, including skills, competencies, and staffing levels?
<--- Score

94. Will a response program recognize when a crisis occurs and provide some level of response?
<--- Score

95. What tools and technologies are needed for a custom Chief investment officer project?
<--- Score

96. Will it solve real problems?
<--- Score

Add up total points for this section:
_ _ _ _ _ = Total points for this section

Divided by: _ _ _ _ _ _ (number of statements answered) = _ _ _ _ _ _ Average score for this section

Transfer your score to the Chief
investment officer Index at the
beginning of the Self-Assessment.

CRITERION #2: DEFINE:

INTENT: Formulate the stakeholder problem. Define the problem, needs and objectives.

In my belief, the answer to this question is clearly defined:

5 Strongly Agree

4 Agree

3 Neutral

2 Disagree

1 Strongly Disagree

1. Are different versions of process maps needed to account for the different types of inputs?
<--- Score

2. How was the 'as is' process map developed, reviewed, verified and validated?
<--- Score

3. What is a worst-case scenario for losses?

<--- Score

4. What sort of initial information to gather?
<--- Score

5. Is there a clear Chief investment officer case definition?
<--- Score

6. Have the customer needs been translated into specific, measurable requirements? How?
<--- Score

7. How do you hand over Chief investment officer context?
<--- Score

8. What intelligence can you gather?
<--- Score

9. Do you have organizational privacy requirements?
<--- Score

10. Is the scope of Chief investment officer defined?
<--- Score

11. What are the requirements for audit information?
<--- Score

12. What is the scope of the Chief investment officer effort?
<--- Score

13. What customer feedback methods were used to solicit their input?

<--- Score

14. Has the direction changed at all during the course of Chief investment officer? If so, when did it change and why?
<--- Score

15. What are the dynamics of the communication plan?
<--- Score

16. Is special Chief investment officer user knowledge required?
<--- Score

17. Is the current 'as is' process being followed? If not, what are the discrepancies?
<--- Score

18. Has/have the customer(s) been identified?
<--- Score

19. Will a Chief investment officer production readiness review be required?
<--- Score

20. Does the team have regular meetings?
<--- Score

21. When is the estimated completion date?
<--- Score

22. How and when will the baselines be defined?
<--- Score

23. What information do you gather?

<--- Score

24. How do you manage scope?
<--- Score

25. Has everyone on the team, including the team leaders, been properly trained?
<--- Score

26. How does the Chief investment officer manager ensure against scope creep?
<--- Score

27. Do you all define Chief investment officer in the same way?
<--- Score

28. How can the value of Chief investment officer be defined?
<--- Score

29. Who approved the Chief investment officer scope?
<--- Score

30. What is the scope of the Chief investment officer work?
<--- Score

31. What knowledge or experience is required?
<--- Score

32. What information should you gather?
<--- Score

33. How do you manage changes in Chief investment officer requirements?

<--- Score

34. How are consistent Chief investment officer definitions important?
<--- Score

35. When are meeting minutes sent out? Who is on the distribution list?
<--- Score

36. What system do you use for gathering Chief investment officer information?
<--- Score

37. How would you define the culture at your organization, how susceptible is it to Chief investment officer changes?
<--- Score

38. How do you gather Chief investment officer requirements?
<--- Score

39. What is the definition of success?
<--- Score

40. Are roles and responsibilities formally defined?
<--- Score

41. What are the boundaries of the scope? What is in bounds and what is not? What is the start point? What is the stop point?
<--- Score

42. What sources do you use to gather information for a Chief investment officer study?

<--- Score

43. Have all of the relationships been defined properly?
<--- Score

44. Are approval levels defined for contracts and supplements to contracts?
<--- Score

45. Is there any additional Chief investment officer definition of success?
<--- Score

46. How would you define Chief investment officer leadership?
<--- Score

47. Is the improvement team aware of the different versions of a process: what they think it is vs. what it actually is vs. what it should be vs. what it could be?
<--- Score

48. What constraints exist that might impact the team?
<--- Score

49. How is the team tracking and documenting its work?
<--- Score

50. What defines best in class?
<--- Score

51. Why are you doing Chief investment officer and what is the scope?

<--- Score

52. Are required metrics defined, what are they?
<--- Score

53. Is Chief investment officer linked to key
stakeholder goals and objectives?
<--- Score

54. Is the work to date meeting requirements?
<--- Score

55. What are the rough order estimates on cost
savings/opportunities that Chief investment officer
brings?
<--- Score

56. Has a project plan, Gantt chart, or similar been
developed/completed?
<--- Score

**57. What is the definition of Chief investment
officer excellence?**
<--- Score

58. Is there a Chief investment officer management
charter, including stakeholder case, problem and
goal statements, scope, milestones, roles and
responsibilities, communication plan?
<--- Score

59. What scope do you want your strategy to cover?
<--- Score

**60. What are the record-keeping requirements of
Chief investment officer activities?**

<--- Score

61. What key stakeholder process output measure(s) does Chief investment officer leverage and how?
<--- Score

62. Has a high-level 'as is' process map been completed, verified and validated?
<--- Score

63. Is there a critical path to deliver Chief investment officer results?
<--- Score

64. How do you gather the stories?
<--- Score

65. What is out-of-scope initially?
<--- Score

66. Is scope creep really all bad news?
<--- Score

67. What specifically is the problem? Where does it occur? When does it occur? What is its extent?
<--- Score

68. Has a team charter been developed and communicated?
<--- Score

69. Do the problem and goal statements meet the SMART criteria (specific, measurable, attainable, relevant, and time-bound)?
<--- Score

70. Who is gathering Chief investment officer information?
<--- Score

71. What are (control) requirements for Chief investment officer Information?
<--- Score

72. What are the tasks and definitions?
<--- Score

73. What was the context?
<--- Score

74. Scope of sensitive information?
<--- Score

75. Is there a completed, verified, and validated high-level 'as is' (not 'should be' or 'could be') stakeholder process map?
<--- Score

76. Are task requirements clearly defined?
<--- Score

77. What are the core elements of the Chief investment officer business case?
<--- Score

78. Are there any constraints known that bear on the ability to perform Chief investment officer work? How is the team addressing them?
<--- Score

79. What is in the scope and what is not in scope?
<--- Score

80. What scope to assess?
<--- Score

81. How do you manage unclear Chief investment officer requirements?
<--- Score

82. Are the Chief investment officer requirements testable?
<--- Score

83. What is in scope?
<--- Score

84. What are the Chief investment officer use cases?
<--- Score

85. What is the worst case scenario?
<--- Score

86. How do you build the right business case?
<--- Score

87. Are there different segments of customers?
<--- Score

88. Has a Chief investment officer requirement not been met?
<--- Score

89. Who is gathering information?
<--- Score

90. Is Chief investment officer currently on schedule according to the plan?

<--- Score

91. Has anyone else (internal or external to the group) attempted to solve this problem or a similar one before? If so, what knowledge can be leveraged from these previous efforts?
<--- Score

92. How do you keep key subject matter experts in the loop?
<--- Score

93. How do you gather requirements?
<--- Score

94. What is out of scope?
<--- Score

95. What Chief investment officer requirements should be gathered?
<--- Score

96. In what way can you redefine the criteria of choice clients have in your category in your favor?
<--- Score

97. How have you defined all Chief investment officer requirements first?
<--- Score

98. The political context: who holds power?
<--- Score

99. How will the Chief investment officer team and the group measure complete success of Chief investment officer?

<--- Score

100. Do you have a Chief investment officer success story or case study ready to tell and share?
<--- Score

101. What are the Roles and Responsibilities for each team member and its leadership? Where is this documented?
<--- Score

102. Does the scope remain the same?
<--- Score

103. Has the improvement team collected the 'voice of the customer' (obtained feedback – qualitative and quantitative)?
<--- Score

104. Is the team adequately staffed with the desired cross-functionality? If not, what additional resources are available to the team?
<--- Score

105. What is the context?
<--- Score

106. Are accountability and ownership for Chief investment officer clearly defined?
<--- Score

107. What baselines are required to be defined and managed?
<--- Score

108. How did the Chief investment officer manager

receive input to the development of a Chief investment officer improvement plan and the estimated completion dates/times of each activity?
<--- Score

109. Is there a completed SIPOC representation, describing the Suppliers, Inputs, Process, Outputs, and Customers?
<--- Score

110. How do you catch Chief investment officer definition inconsistencies?
<--- Score

111. What Chief investment officer services do you require?
<--- Score

112. Is Chief investment officer required?
<--- Score

113. Is data collected and displayed to better understand customer(s) critical needs and requirements.
<--- Score

114. Have specific policy objectives been defined?
<--- Score

115. Are the Chief investment officer requirements complete?
<--- Score

116. What gets examined?
<--- Score

117. Who defines (or who defined) the rules and roles?
<--- Score

118. What are the Chief investment officer tasks and definitions?
<--- Score

119. Are audit criteria, scope, frequency and methods defined?
<--- Score

120. How often are the team meetings?
<--- Score

121. Is the Chief investment officer scope complete and appropriately sized?
<--- Score

122. What critical content must be communicated – who, what, when, where, and how?
<--- Score

123. Is it clearly defined in and to your organization what you do?
<--- Score

124. What is the scope of Chief investment officer?
<--- Score

125. Is there regularly 100% attendance at the team meetings? If not, have appointed substitutes attended to preserve cross-functionality and full representation?
<--- Score

126. What happens if Chief investment officer's scope

changes?
<--- Score

127. What are the compelling stakeholder reasons for embarking on Chief investment officer?
<--- Score

128. Where can you gather more information?
<--- Score

129. Are resources adequate for the scope?
<--- Score

130. Have all basic functions of Chief investment officer been defined?
<--- Score

131. How do you think the partners involved in Chief investment officer would have defined success?
<--- Score

132. Is the Chief investment officer scope manageable?
<--- Score

133. What would be the goal or target for a Chief investment officer's improvement team?
<--- Score

134. Has the Chief investment officer work been fairly and/or equitably divided and delegated among team members who are qualified and capable to perform the work? Has everyone contributed?
<--- Score

135. Who are the Chief investment officer

improvement team members, including Management Leads and Coaches?

<--- Score

136. When is/was the Chief investment officer start date?

<--- Score

137. If substitutes have been appointed, have they been briefed on the Chief investment officer goals and received regular communications as to the progress to date?

<--- Score

138. How will variation in the actual durations of each activity be dealt with to ensure that the expected Chief investment officer results are met?

<--- Score

Add up total points for this section:
_____ = Total points for this section

Divided by: _____ (number of statements answered) = _____
Average score for this section

Transfer your score to the Chief investment officer Index at the beginning of the Self-Assessment.

CRITERION #3: MEASURE:

INTENT: Gather the correct data. Measure the current performance and evolution of the situation.

In my belief, the answer to this question is clearly defined:

5 Strongly Agree

4 Agree

3 Neutral

2 Disagree

1 Strongly Disagree

1. What are your primary costs, revenues, assets?
<--- Score

2. Do you have an issue in getting priority?
<--- Score

3. Why a Chief investment officer focus?
<--- Score

4. Does a Chief investment officer quantification method exist?

<--- Score

5. What is the total cost related to deploying Chief investment officer, including any consulting or professional services?

<--- Score

6. Do you have a flow diagram of what happens?

<--- Score

7. Are there measurements based on task performance?

<--- Score

8. What is your decision requirements diagram?

<--- Score

9. Have design-to-cost goals been established?

<--- Score

10. How can you reduce costs?

<--- Score

11. How do you aggregate measures across priorities?

<--- Score

12. How frequently do you verify your Chief investment officer strategy?

<--- Score

13. What do people want to verify?

<--- Score

14. Who is involved in verifying compliance?

<--- Score

15. How will success or failure be measured?
<--- Score

16. Did you tackle the cause or the symptom?
<--- Score

17. How is the value delivered by Chief investment officer being measured?
<--- Score

18. Does the Chief investment officer task fit the client's priorities?
<--- Score

19. What measurements are possible, practicable and meaningful?
<--- Score

20. What can be used to verify compliance?
<--- Score

21. What potential environmental factors impact the Chief investment officer effort?
<--- Score

22. How frequently do you track Chief investment officer measures?
<--- Score

23. What are the costs and benefits?
<--- Score

24. What causes extra work or rework?
<--- Score

25. Does management have the right priorities among projects?

<--- Score

26. Are there competing Chief investment officer priorities?

<--- Score

27. What are your key Chief investment officer organizational performance measures, including key short and longer-term financial measures?

<--- Score

28. Is a follow-up focused external Chief investment officer review required?

<--- Score

29. What happens if cost savings do not materialize?

<--- Score

30. What are your customers expectations and measures?

<--- Score

31. What are the Chief investment officer investment costs?

<--- Score

32. How do you verify performance?

<--- Score

33. When are costs are incurred?

<--- Score

34. Are actual costs in line with budgeted costs?

<--- Score

35. How are you verifying it?
<--- Score

36. Was a life-cycle cost analysis performed?
<--- Score

37. What is the total fixed cost?
<--- Score

38. Is it possible to estimate the impact of unanticipated complexity such as wrong or failed assumptions, feedback, etcetera on proposed reforms?
<--- Score

39. What does losing customers cost your organization?
<--- Score

40. At what cost?
<--- Score

41. What is measured? Why?
<--- Score

42. Where is the cost?
<--- Score

43. What are hidden Chief investment officer quality costs?
<--- Score

44. How do you verify the authenticity of the data and information used?

<--- Score

45. What does verifying compliance entail?
<--- Score

46. What evidence is there and what is measured?
<--- Score

47. What is the cause of any Chief investment officer gaps?
<--- Score

48. What causes innovation to fail or succeed in your organization?
<--- Score

49. How do you control the overall costs of your work processes?
<--- Score

50. How much does it cost?
<--- Score

51. What is your cost benefit analysis?
<--- Score

52. How do you measure lifecycle phases?
<--- Score

53. Are missed Chief investment officer opportunities costing your organization money?
<--- Score

54. How do you stay flexible and focused to recognize larger Chief investment officer results?
<--- Score

55. How will you measure your Chief investment officer effectiveness?
<--- Score

56. What disadvantage does this cause for the user?
<--- Score

57. Are you aware of what could cause a problem?
<--- Score

58. Are there any easy-to-implement alternatives to Chief investment officer? Sometimes other solutions are available that do not require the cost implications of a full-blown project?
<--- Score

59. How do you verify if Chief investment officer is built right?
<--- Score

60. What are the types and number of measures to use?
<--- Score

61. How do you verify the Chief investment officer requirements quality?
<--- Score

62. Are the measurements objective?
<--- Score

63. What are predictive Chief investment officer analytics?
<--- Score

64. How do you measure success?
<--- Score

65. How are measurements made?
<--- Score

66. What would it cost to replace your technology?
<--- Score

67. Was a business case (cost/benefit) developed?
<--- Score

68. Do you aggressively reward and promote the people who have the biggest impact on creating excellent Chief investment officer services/ products?
<--- Score

69. What are you verifying?
<--- Score

70. How to cause the change?
<--- Score

71. How will costs be allocated?
<--- Score

72. Has a cost center been established?
<--- Score

73. Do the benefits outweigh the costs?
<--- Score

74. What are the operational costs after Chief investment officer deployment?
<--- Score

75. Are the Chief investment officer benefits worth its costs?

<--- Score

76. What drives O&M cost?

<--- Score

77. Is there an opportunity to verify requirements?

<--- Score

78. What measurements are being captured?

<--- Score

79. Are indirect costs charged to the Chief investment officer program?

<--- Score

80. Is the scope of Chief investment officer cost analysis cost-effective?

<--- Score

81. How do you verify your resources?

<--- Score

82. Are you able to realize any cost savings?

<--- Score

83. Where can you go to verify the info?

<--- Score

84. What causes investor action?

<--- Score

85. What would be a real cause for concern?

<--- Score

86. Have you made assumptions about the shape of the future, particularly its impact on your customers and competitors?
<--- Score

87. How do you verify Chief investment officer completeness and accuracy?
<--- Score

88. How can you manage cost down?
<--- Score

89. How do you measure variability?
<--- Score

90. Have you included everything in your Chief investment officer cost models?
<--- Score

91. What are the Chief investment officer key cost drivers?
<--- Score

92. What are the uncertainties surrounding estimates of impact?
<--- Score

93. What is the root cause(s) of the problem?
<--- Score

94. What are your operating costs?
<--- Score

95. What are the costs?
<--- Score

96. Is the solution cost-effective?

<--- Score

97. How can you measure the performance?

<--- Score

98. What does your operating model cost?

<--- Score

99. The approach of traditional Chief investment officer works for detail complexity but is focused on a systematic approach rather than an understanding of the nature of systems themselves, what approach will permit your organization to deal with the kind of unpredictable emergent behaviors that dynamic complexity can introduce?

<--- Score

100. What could cause you to change course?

<--- Score

101. Why do the measurements/indicators matter?

<--- Score

102. Are Chief investment officer vulnerabilities categorized and prioritized?

<--- Score

103. Are the units of measure consistent?

<--- Score

104. What details are required of the Chief investment officer cost structure?

<--- Score

105. What are the costs of reform?
<--- Score

106. How do your measurements capture actionable Chief investment officer information for use in exceeding your customers expectations and securing your customers engagement?
<--- Score

107. What are the estimated costs of proposed changes?
<--- Score

108. What is your Chief investment officer quality cost segregation study?
<--- Score

109. What methods are feasible and acceptable to estimate the impact of reforms?
<--- Score

110. Among the Chief investment officer product and service cost to be estimated, which is considered hardest to estimate?
<--- Score

111. When should you bother with diagrams?
<--- Score

112. What harm might be caused?
<--- Score

113. How can a Chief investment officer test verify your ideas or assumptions?
<--- Score

114. What is an unallowable cost?

<--- Score

115. How do you verify and develop ideas and innovations?

<--- Score

116. Is the cost worth the Chief investment officer effort ?

<--- Score

117. What are the current costs of the Chief investment officer process?

<--- Score

118. What users will be impacted?

<--- Score

119. What is the cost of rework?

<--- Score

120. How will the Chief investment officer data be analyzed?

<--- Score

121. Do you have any cost Chief investment officer limitation requirements?

<--- Score

122. Which measures and indicators matter?

<--- Score

123. How can you reduce the costs of obtaining inputs?

<--- Score

124. How will you measure success?
<--- Score

125. How will your organization measure success?
<--- Score

126. Are you taking your company in the direction of better and revenue or cheaper and cost?
<--- Score

127. Which Chief investment officer impacts are significant?
<--- Score

128. What relevant entities could be measured?
<--- Score

129. What does a Test Case verify?
<--- Score

130. What could cause delays in the schedule?
<--- Score

131. Are supply costs steady or fluctuating?
<--- Score

132. How is progress measured?
<--- Score

133. How will effects be measured?
<--- Score

134. How long to keep data and how to manage retention costs?
<--- Score

135. How can you measure Chief investment officer in a systematic way?
<--- Score

136. Where is it measured?
<--- Score

137. How do you prevent mis-estimating cost?
<--- Score

138. How will measures be used to manage and adapt?
<--- Score

139. How are costs allocated?
<--- Score

140. Why do you expend time and effort to implement measurement, for whom?
<--- Score

141. Will Chief investment officer have an impact on current business continuity, disaster recovery processes and/or infrastructure?
<--- Score

Add up total points for this section:
_____ = Total points for this section

Divided by: _____ (number of statements answered) = _____
Average score for this section

Transfer your score to the Chief investment officer Index at the beginning of the Self-Assessment.

CRITERION #4: ANALYZE:

INTENT: Analyze causes, assumptions and hypotheses.

In my belief, the answer to this question is clearly defined:

5 Strongly Agree

4 Agree

3 Neutral

2 Disagree

1 Strongly Disagree

1. Have the problem and goal statements been updated to reflect the additional knowledge gained from the analyze phase?
<--- Score

2. What successful thing are you doing today that may be blinding you to new growth opportunities?
<--- Score

3. What is your organizations process which leads to

recognition of value generation?
<--- Score

4. Is the suppliers process defined and controlled?
<--- Score

5. What methods do you use to gather Chief investment officer data?
<--- Score

6. Where is the data coming from to measure compliance?
<--- Score

7. What data is gathered?
<--- Score

8. How do you implement and manage your work processes to ensure that they meet design requirements?
<--- Score

9. Do staff qualifications match your project?
<--- Score

10. Were Pareto charts (or similar) used to portray the 'heavy hitters' (or key sources of variation)?
<--- Score

11. Identify an operational issue in your organization, for example, could a particular task be done more quickly or more efficiently by Chief investment officer?
<--- Score

12. How is the data gathered?

<--- Score

13. What are the personnel training and qualifications required?
<--- Score

14. Do your leaders quickly bounce back from setbacks?
<--- Score

15. How was the detailed process map generated, verified, and validated?
<--- Score

16. Who will gather what data?
<--- Score

17. What were the financial benefits resulting from any 'ground fruit or low-hanging fruit' (quick fixes)?
<--- Score

18. Do quality systems drive continuous improvement?
<--- Score

19. What process improvements will be needed?
<--- Score

20. Have any additional benefits been identified that will result from closing all or most of the gaps?
<--- Score

21. Did any additional data need to be collected?
<--- Score

22. How does the organization define, manage,

and improve its Chief investment officer processes?

<--- Score

23. What are the Chief investment officer business drivers?

<--- Score

24. Are all staff in core Chief investment officer subjects Highly Qualified?

<--- Score

25. Think about some of the processes you undertake within your organization, which do you own?

<--- Score

26. Record-keeping requirements flow from the records needed as inputs, outputs, controls and for transformation of a Chief investment officer process, are the records needed as inputs to the Chief investment officer process available?

<--- Score

27. How much data can be collected in the given timeframe?

<--- Score

28. Is the performance gap determined?

<--- Score

29. What qualifies as competition?

<--- Score

30. Has data output been validated?

<--- Score

31. Has an output goal been set?
<--- Score

32. Have you defined which data is gathered how?
<--- Score

33. Can you add value to the current Chief investment officer decision-making process (largely qualitative) by incorporating uncertainty modeling (more quantitative)?
<--- Score

34. How will the change process be managed?
<--- Score

35. Who gets your output?
<--- Score

36. How many input/output points does it require?
<--- Score

37. Are gaps between current performance and the goal performance identified?
<--- Score

38. How often will data be collected for measures?
<--- Score

39. Is the required Chief investment officer data gathered?
<--- Score

40. What qualifications and skills do you need?
<--- Score

41. What are your outputs?

<--- Score

42. Are you missing Chief investment officer opportunities?
<--- Score

43. What output to create?
<--- Score

44. How do you use Chief investment officer data and information to support organizational decision making and innovation?
<--- Score

45. What are the disruptive Chief investment officer technologies that enable your organization to radically change your business processes?
<--- Score

46. What are your key performance measures or indicators and in-process measures for the control and improvement of your Chief investment officer processes?
<--- Score

47. How do you define collaboration and team output?
<--- Score

48. What Chief investment officer metrics are outputs of the process?
<--- Score

49. What are your current levels and trends in key Chief investment officer measures or indicators of product and process performance that are important

to and directly serve your customers?
<--- Score

50. A compounding model resolution with available relevant data can often provide insight towards a solution methodology; which Chief investment officer models, tools and techniques are necessary?
<--- Score

51. What are your current levels and trends in key measures or indicators of Chief investment officer product and process performance that are important to and directly serve your customers? How do these results compare with the performance of your competitors and other organizations with similar offerings?
<--- Score

52. What tools were used to generate the list of possible causes?
<--- Score

53. What, related to, Chief investment officer processes does your organization outsource?
<--- Score

54. What qualifications do Chief investment officer leaders need?
<--- Score

55. What is the Chief investment officer Driver?
<--- Score

56. Did any value-added analysis or 'lean thinking' take place to identify some of the gaps shown on the 'as is' process map?

<--- Score

57. Do your employees have the opportunity to do what they do best everyday?
<--- Score

58. Do several people in different organizational units assist with the Chief investment officer process?
<--- Score

59. Is the final output clearly identified?
<--- Score

60. Who owns what data?
<--- Score

61. How do you measure the operational performance of your key work systems and processes, including productivity, cycle time, and other appropriate measures of process effectiveness, efficiency, and innovation?
<--- Score

62. How has the Chief investment officer data been gathered?
<--- Score

63. Do your contracts/agreements contain data security obligations?
<--- Score

64. What conclusions were drawn from the team's data collection and analysis? How did the team reach these conclusions?
<--- Score

65. Who is involved with workflow mapping?

<--- Score

66. Who qualifies to gain access to data?

<--- Score

67. What controls do you have in place to protect data?

<--- Score

68. What resources go in to get the desired output?

<--- Score

69. Are Chief investment officer changes recognized early enough to be approved through the regular process?

<--- Score

70. Were any designed experiments used to generate additional insight into the data analysis?

<--- Score

71. What Chief investment officer data should be managed?

<--- Score

72. Are your outputs consistent?

<--- Score

73. How is the way you as the leader think and process information affecting your organizational culture?

<--- Score

74. What are your best practices for minimizing Chief investment officer project risk, while demonstrating incremental value and quick wins

throughout the Chief investment officer project lifecycle?
<--- Score

75. What qualifications are necessary?
<--- Score

76. Are all team members qualified for all tasks?
<--- Score

77. What is the Value Stream Mapping?
<--- Score

78. What are the necessary qualifications?
<--- Score

79. Do you, as a leader, bounce back quickly from setbacks?
<--- Score

80. What are the key elements of your Chief investment officer performance improvement system, including your evaluation, organizational learning, and innovation processes?
<--- Score

81. What are evaluation criteria for the output?
<--- Score

82. Think about the functions involved in your Chief investment officer project, what processes flow from these functions?
<--- Score

83. What will drive Chief investment officer change?

<--- Score

84. Was a detailed process map created to amplify critical steps of the 'as is' stakeholder process?
<--- Score

85. Were there any improvement opportunities identified from the process analysis?
<--- Score

86. What are your Chief investment officer processes?
<--- Score

87. What process should you select for improvement?
<--- Score

88. What is the oversight process?
<--- Score

89. What are the best opportunities for value improvement?
<--- Score

90. What Chief investment officer data will be collected?
<--- Score

91. What other organizational variables, such as reward systems or communication systems, affect the performance of this Chief investment officer process?
<--- Score

92. How difficult is it to qualify what Chief investment

officer ROI is?

<--- Score

93. What are the Chief investment officer design outputs?

<--- Score

94. What are the revised rough estimates of the financial savings/opportunity for Chief investment officer improvements?

<--- Score

95. What types of data do your Chief investment officer indicators require?

<--- Score

96. What kind of crime could a potential new hire have committed that would not only not disqualify him/her from being hired by your organization, but would actually indicate that he/she might be a particularly good fit?

<--- Score

97. How do you ensure that the Chief investment officer opportunity is realistic?

<--- Score

98. What other jobs or tasks affect the performance of the steps in the Chief investment officer process?

<--- Score

99. How is Chief investment officer data gathered?

<--- Score

100. Is the gap/opportunity displayed and

communicated in financial terms?
<--- Score

101. What quality tools were used to get through the analyze phase?
<--- Score

102. Do you have the authority to produce the output?
<--- Score

103. How can risk management be tied procedurally to process elements?
<--- Score

104. Should you invest in industry-recognized qualifications?
<--- Score

105. Is there any way to speed up the process?
<--- Score

106. What is the complexity of the output produced?
<--- Score

107. What tools were used to narrow the list of possible causes?
<--- Score

108. How is the Chief investment officer Value Stream Mapping managed?
<--- Score

109. How do mission and objectives affect the Chief investment officer processes of your organization?

<--- Score

110. Is there a strict change management process?
<--- Score

111. Is data and process analysis, root cause analysis and quantifying the gap/opportunity in place?
<--- Score

112. What were the crucial 'moments of truth' on the process map?
<--- Score

113. Where can you get qualified talent today?
<--- Score

114. What do you need to qualify?
<--- Score

115. What is the cost of poor quality as supported by the team's analysis?
<--- Score

116. What systems/processes must you excel at?
<--- Score

117. How do you identify specific Chief investment officer investment opportunities and emerging trends?
<--- Score

118. Do you understand your management processes today?
<--- Score

119. What is your organizations system for

selecting qualified vendors?
<--- Score

120. Where is Chief investment officer data gathered?
<--- Score

121. Is there an established change management process?
<--- Score

122. What does the data say about the performance of the stakeholder process?
<--- Score

123. Was a cause-and-effect diagram used to explore the different types of causes (or sources of variation)?
<--- Score

124. What did the team gain from developing a sub-process map?
<--- Score

125. What Chief investment officer data should be collected?
<--- Score

126. What Chief investment officer data do you gather or use now?
<--- Score

127. When should a process be art not science?
<--- Score

128. What training and qualifications will you need?
<--- Score

129. What data do you need to collect?
<--- Score

130. Who is involved in the management review process?
<--- Score

131. What information qualified as important?
<--- Score

132. What internal processes need improvement?
<--- Score

133. What qualifications are needed?
<--- Score

134. What is the output?
<--- Score

135. Is the Chief investment officer process severely broken such that a re-design is necessary?
<--- Score

136. Which Chief investment officer data should be retained?
<--- Score

Add up total points for this section:
_ _ _ _ _ = Total points for this section

Divided by: _ _ _ _ _ _ (number of statements answered) = _ _ _ _ _ _ Average score for this section

Transfer your score to the Chief

investment officer Index at the
beginning of the Self-Assessment.

CRITERION #5: IMPROVE:

INTENT: Develop a practical solution.
Innovate, establish and test the
solution and to measure the results.

In my belief, the answer to this
question is clearly defined:

5 Strongly Agree

4 Agree

3 Neutral

2 Disagree

1 Strongly Disagree

1. Is any Chief investment officer documentation
required?
<--- Score

2. Do you combine technical expertise with business
knowledge and Chief investment officer Key topics
include lifecycles, development approaches,
requirements and how to make a business case?
<--- Score

3. Who do you report Chief investment officer results to?
<--- Score

4. If you could go back in time five years, what decision would you make differently? What is your best guess as to what decision you're making today you might regret five years from now?
<--- Score

5. Are risk triggers captured?
<--- Score

6. What are the expected Chief investment officer results?
<--- Score

7. What can you do to improve?
<--- Score

8. How risky is your organization?
<--- Score

9. What do you want to improve?
<--- Score

10. Who will be responsible for making the decisions to include or exclude requested changes once Chief investment officer is underway?
<--- Score

11. What is the Chief investment officer's sustainability risk?
<--- Score

12. Who are the people involved in developing and implementing Chief investment officer?
<--- Score

13. Is there a small-scale pilot for proposed improvement(s)? What conclusions were drawn from the outcomes of a pilot?
<--- Score

14. What is the implementation plan?
<--- Score

15. Is supporting Chief investment officer documentation required?
<--- Score

16. How will you measure the results?
<--- Score

17. How will you know that a change is an improvement?
<--- Score

18. Is the scope clearly documented?
<--- Score

19. Is the Chief investment officer documentation thorough?
<--- Score

20. What practices helps your organization to develop its capacity to recognize patterns?
<--- Score

21. Who will be responsible for documenting the Chief investment officer requirements in detail?

<--- Score

22. Are the key business and technology risks being managed?
<--- Score

23. What is the risk?
<--- Score

24. What alternative responses are available to manage risk?
<--- Score

25. How do you mitigate Chief investment officer risk?
<--- Score

26. What were the criteria for evaluating a Chief investment officer pilot?
<--- Score

27. What are your current levels and trends in key measures or indicators of workforce and leader development?
<--- Score

28. What strategies for Chief investment officer improvement are successful?
<--- Score

29. How do you improve productivity?
<--- Score

30. For decision problems, how do you develop a decision statement?
<--- Score

31. How does the team improve its work?
<--- Score

32. Do you need to do a usability evaluation?
<--- Score

33. Is the solution technically practical?
<--- Score

34. What actually has to improve and by how much?
<--- Score

35. How do you keep improving Chief investment officer?
<--- Score

36. Are events managed to resolution?
<--- Score

37. How do you improve your likelihood of success ?
<--- Score

38. How do you improve Chief investment officer service perception, and satisfaction?
<--- Score

39. What are the Chief investment officer security risks?
<--- Score

40. Which of the recognised risks out of all risks can be most likely transferred?
<--- Score

41. Who should make the Chief investment officer

decisions?

<--- Score

42. Have you identified breakpoints and/or risk tolerances that will trigger broad consideration of a potential need for intervention or modification of strategy?

<--- Score

43. Will the controls trigger any other risks?

<--- Score

44. Are the most efficient solutions problem-specific?

<--- Score

45. What does the 'should be' process map/design look like?

<--- Score

46. Where do the Chief investment officer decisions reside?

<--- Score

47. Do you cover the five essential competencies: Communication, Collaboration,Innovation, Adaptability, and Leadership that improve an organizations ability to leverage the new Chief investment officer in a volatile global economy?

<--- Score

48. Was a Chief investment officer charter developed?

<--- Score

49. When you map the key players in your own work and the types/domains of relationships with them, which relationships do you find easy and which

challenging, and why?
<--- Score

50. Does a good decision guarantee a good outcome?
<--- Score

51. How risky is your organization?
<--- Score

52. Who makes the Chief investment officer decisions in your organization?
<--- Score

53. How are policy decisions made and where?
<--- Score

54. How do you go about comparing Chief investment officer approaches/solutions?
<--- Score

55. How do you define the solutions' scope?
<--- Score

56. Do the viable solutions scale to future needs?
<--- Score

57. How do the Chief investment officer results compare with the performance of your competitors and other organizations with similar offerings?
<--- Score

58. What are the implications of the one critical Chief investment officer decision 10 minutes, 10 months, and 10 years from now?
<--- Score

59. How significant is the improvement in the eyes of the end user?
<--- Score

60. Who are the key stakeholders for the Chief investment officer evaluation?
<--- Score

61. How do you measure improved Chief investment officer service perception, and satisfaction?
<--- Score

62. What resources are required for the improvement efforts?
<--- Score

63. How are Chief investment officer risks managed?
<--- Score

64. Does the goal represent a desired result that can be measured?
<--- Score

65. Have you achieved Chief investment officer improvements?
<--- Score

66. What is Chief investment officer risk?
<--- Score

67. Are risk management tasks balanced centrally and locally?
<--- Score

68. Do vendor agreements bring new compliance risk
?
<--- Score

69. What error proofing will be done to address some
of the discrepancies observed in the 'as is' process?
<--- Score

70. Is the Chief investment officer risk managed?
<--- Score

71. Where do you need Chief investment officer
improvement?
<--- Score

72. Who manages Chief investment officer risk?
<--- Score

73. How does your organization evaluate strategic
Chief investment officer success?
<--- Score

74. Who manages supplier risk management in your
organization?
<--- Score

75. Would you develop a Chief investment officer
Communication Strategy?
<--- Score

76. What to do with the results or outcomes of
measurements?
<--- Score

77. For estimation problems, how do you develop an
estimation statement?

<--- Score

78. How will you know that you have improved?
<--- Score

79. What tools do you use once you have decided on a Chief investment officer strategy and more importantly how do you choose?
<--- Score

80. What needs improvement? Why?
<--- Score

81. Can the solution be designed and implemented within an acceptable time period?
<--- Score

82. Who controls the risk?
<--- Score

83. Who are the Chief investment officer decision makers?
<--- Score

84. Which Chief investment officer solution is appropriate?
<--- Score

85. What communications are necessary to support the implementation of the solution?
<--- Score

86. Were any criteria developed to assist the team in testing and evaluating potential solutions?
<--- Score

87. Can you identify any significant risks or exposures to Chief investment officer third- parties (vendors, service providers, alliance partners etc) that concern you?
<--- Score

88. How will you recognize and celebrate results?
<--- Score

89. Why improve in the first place?
<--- Score

90. Risk Identification: What are the possible risk events your organization faces in relation to Chief investment officer?
<--- Score

91. To what extent does management recognize Chief investment officer as a tool to increase the results?
<--- Score

92. Explorations of the frontiers of Chief investment officer will help you build influence, improve Chief investment officer, optimize decision making, and sustain change, what is your approach?
<--- Score

93. What is the magnitude of the improvements?
<--- Score

94. Who will be using the results of the measurement activities?
<--- Score

95. How can you improve Chief investment officer?

<--- Score

96. How can you improve performance?
<--- Score

97. What tools were used to tap into the creativity and encourage 'outside the box' thinking?
<--- Score

98. Who controls key decisions that will be made?
<--- Score

99. What assumptions are made about the solution and approach?
<--- Score

100. What risks do you need to manage?
<--- Score

101. How is knowledge sharing about risk management improved?
<--- Score

102. Who are the Chief investment officer decision-makers?
<--- Score

103. What are the concrete Chief investment officer results?
<--- Score

104. How can the phases of Chief investment officer development be identified?
<--- Score

105. How do you manage Chief investment officer

risk?

<--- Score

106. How do you decide how much to remunerate an employee?

<--- Score

107. What tools were used to evaluate the potential solutions?

<--- Score

108. How can skill-level changes improve Chief investment officer?

<--- Score

109. Are decisions made in a timely manner?

<--- Score

110. Is Chief investment officer documentation maintained?

<--- Score

111. Is there a cost/benefit analysis of optimal solution(s)?

<--- Score

112. What should a proof of concept or pilot accomplish?

<--- Score

113. What attendant changes will need to be made to ensure that the solution is successful?

<--- Score

114. Was a pilot designed for the proposed solution(s)?

<--- Score

115. What are the affordable Chief investment officer risks?
<--- Score

116. Risk factors: what are the characteristics of Chief investment officer that make it risky?
<--- Score

117. Is the Chief investment officer solution sustainable?
<--- Score

118. How is continuous improvement applied to risk management?
<--- Score

119. How do you measure progress and evaluate training effectiveness?
<--- Score

120. What criteria will you use to assess your Chief investment officer risks?
<--- Score

121. What is Chief investment officer's impact on utilizing the best solution(s)?
<--- Score

122. What Chief investment officer improvements can be made?
<--- Score

123. How can you better manage risk?
<--- Score

124. Is risk periodically assessed?
<--- Score

125. Risk events: what are the things that could go wrong?
<--- Score

126. What were the underlying assumptions on the cost-benefit analysis?
<--- Score

127. Do those selected for the Chief investment officer team have a good general understanding of what Chief investment officer is all about?
<--- Score

128. How scalable is your Chief investment officer solution?
<--- Score

129. How do you deal with Chief investment officer risk?
<--- Score

130. Are you assessing Chief investment officer and risk?
<--- Score

131. How do you manage and improve your Chief investment officer work systems to deliver customer value and achieve organizational success and sustainability?
<--- Score

132. What is the team's contingency plan for potential

problems occurring in implementation?
<--- Score

133. Chief investment officer risk decisions: whose call
Is It?
<--- Score

134. What improvements have been achieved?
<--- Score

135. Can you integrate quality management and risk
management?
<--- Score

136. What tools were most useful during the improve
phase?
<--- Score

137. Is the measure of success for Chief investment
officer understandable to a variety of people?
<--- Score

138. What area needs the greatest improvement?
<--- Score

139. Do you have the optimal project management
team structure?
<--- Score

140. How will you know when its improved?
<--- Score

**141. At what point will vulnerability assessments
be performed once Chief investment officer is put
into production (e.g., ongoing Risk Management
after implementation)?**

<--- Score

142. What lessons, if any, from a pilot were incorporated into the design of the full-scale solution?
<--- Score

Add up total points for this section:
_ _ _ _ _ = Total points for this section

Divided by: _ _ _ _ _ _ (number of
statements answered) = _ _ _ _ _ _
Average score for this section

Transfer your score to the Chief
investment officer Index at the
beginning of the Self-Assessment.

CRITERION #6: CONTROL:

INTENT: Implement the practical solution. Maintain the performance and correct possible complications.

In my belief, the answer to this question is clearly defined:

5 Strongly Agree

4 Agree

3 Neutral

2 Disagree

1 Strongly Disagree

1. Are you measuring, monitoring and predicting Chief investment officer activities to optimize operations and profitability, and enhancing outcomes?
<--- Score

2. Who sets the Chief investment officer standards?
<--- Score

3. Does the response plan contain a definite closed loop continual improvement scheme (e.g., plan-do-check-act)?

<--- Score

4. How do controls support value?

<--- Score

5. What is the control/monitoring plan?

<--- Score

6. What is the standard for acceptable Chief investment officer performance?

<--- Score

7. How do senior leaders actions reflect a commitment to the organizations Chief investment officer values?

<--- Score

8. How widespread is its use?

<--- Score

9. How do you plan on providing proper recognition and disclosure of supporting companies?

<--- Score

10. How will report readings be checked to effectively monitor performance?

<--- Score

11. How do you plan for the cost of succession?

<--- Score

12. Implementation Planning: is a pilot needed to test the changes before a full roll out occurs?

<--- Score

13. Is there a control plan in place for sustaining improvements (short and long-term)?
<--- Score

14. How likely is the current Chief investment officer plan to come in on schedule or on budget?
<--- Score

15. How will the process owner and team be able to hold the gains?
<--- Score

16. Is there a standardized process?
<--- Score

17. What are your results for key measures or indicators of the accomplishment of your Chief investment officer strategy and action plans, including building and strengthening core competencies?
<--- Score

18. Is knowledge gained on process shared and institutionalized?
<--- Score

19. Where do ideas that reach policy makers and planners as proposals for Chief investment officer strengthening and reform actually originate?
<--- Score

20. How will the day-to-day responsibilities for monitoring and continual improvement be transferred from the improvement team to the

process owner?
<--- Score

21. How do you spread information?
<--- Score

22. How will input, process, and output variables be checked to detect for sub-optimal conditions?
<--- Score

23. How is Chief investment officer project cost planned, managed, monitored?
<--- Score

24. What do your reports reflect?
<--- Score

25. What can you control?
<--- Score

26. Will any special training be provided for results interpretation?
<--- Score

27. In the case of a Chief investment officer project, the criteria for the audit derive from implementation objectives, an audit of a Chief investment officer project involves assessing whether the recommendations outlined for implementation have been met, can you track that any Chief investment officer project is implemented as planned, and is it working?
<--- Score

28. How do you encourage people to take control and responsibility?

<--- Score

29. How will you measure your QA plan's effectiveness?
<--- Score

30. Do the Chief investment officer decisions you make today help people and the planet tomorrow?
<--- Score

31. What are the critical parameters to watch?
<--- Score

32. Against what alternative is success being measured?
<--- Score

33. Is there a recommended audit plan for routine surveillance inspections of Chief investment officer's gains?
<--- Score

34. Are documented procedures clear and easy to follow for the operators?
<--- Score

35. What is the recommended frequency of auditing?
<--- Score

36. You may have created your quality measures at a time when you lacked resources, technology wasn't up to the required standard, or low service levels were the industry norm. Have those circumstances changed?
<--- Score

37. Have new or revised work instructions resulted?
<--- Score

38. What is your plan to assess your security risks?
<--- Score

39. Does job training on the documented procedures need to be part of the process team's education and training?
<--- Score

40. What are the known security controls?
<--- Score

41. Who is the Chief investment officer process owner?
<--- Score

42. Who has control over resources?
<--- Score

43. Is there an action plan in case of emergencies?
<--- Score

44. Is there a Chief investment officer Communication plan covering who needs to get what information when?
<--- Score

45. Are the Chief investment officer standards challenging?
<--- Score

46. How will new or emerging customer needs/ requirements be checked/communicated to orient the process toward meeting the new specifications

and continually reducing variation?
<--- Score

47. Do you monitor the Chief investment officer decisions made and fine tune them as they evolve?
<--- Score

48. What adjustments to the strategies are needed?
<--- Score

49. What are customers monitoring?
<--- Score

50. Who will be in control?
<--- Score

51. Do you monitor the effectiveness of your Chief investment officer activities?
<--- Score

52. How is change control managed?
<--- Score

53. What is your theory of human motivation, and how does your compensation plan fit with that view?
<--- Score

54. Has the improved process and its steps been standardized?
<--- Score

55. Is a response plan in place for when the input, process, or output measures indicate an 'out-of-control' condition?
<--- Score

56. Act/Adjust: What Do you Need to Do Differently?
<--- Score

57. Does a troubleshooting guide exist or is it needed?
<--- Score

58. Has the Chief investment officer value of standards been quantified?
<--- Score

59. What key inputs and outputs are being measured on an ongoing basis?
<--- Score

60. Is a response plan established and deployed?
<--- Score

61. Can support from partners be adjusted?
<--- Score

62. Is reporting being used or needed?
<--- Score

63. What quality tools were useful in the control phase?
<--- Score

64. How do your controls stack up?
<--- Score

65. How will Chief investment officer decisions be made and monitored?
<--- Score

66. Are the planned controls in place?
<--- Score

67. Is there a documented and implemented monitoring plan?
<--- Score

68. What is the best design framework for Chief investment officer organization now that, in a post industrial-age if the top-down, command and control model is no longer relevant?
<--- Score

69. Is new knowledge gained imbedded in the response plan?
<--- Score

70. Are new process steps, standards, and documentation ingrained into normal operations?
<--- Score

71. Are operating procedures consistent?
<--- Score

72. Who controls critical resources?
<--- Score

73. Is the Chief investment officer test/monitoring cost justified?
<--- Score

74. Are the planned controls working?
<--- Score

75. How do you select, collect, align, and integrate Chief investment officer data and information for tracking daily operations and overall organizational performance, including progress relative to strategic

objectives and action plans?

<--- Score

76. Will your goals reflect your program budget?

<--- Score

77. What are you attempting to measure/monitor?

<--- Score

78. What do you stand for--and what are you against?

<--- Score

79. Can you adapt and adjust to changing Chief investment officer situations?

<--- Score

80. Are suggested corrective/restorative actions indicated on the response plan for known causes to problems that might surface?

<--- Score

81. How might the group capture best practices and lessons learned so as to leverage improvements?

<--- Score

82. What other systems, operations, processes, and infrastructures (hiring practices, staffing, training, incentives/rewards, metrics/dashboards/scorecards, etc.) need updates, additions, changes, or deletions in order to facilitate knowledge transfer and improvements?

<--- Score

83. How do you monitor usage and cost?

<--- Score

84. Are controls in place and consistently applied?
<--- Score

85. Are there documented procedures?
<--- Score

86. What should you measure to verify efficiency gains?
<--- Score

87. What should the next improvement project be that is related to Chief investment officer?
<--- Score

88. Are pertinent alerts monitored, analyzed and distributed to appropriate personnel?
<--- Score

89. How do you establish and deploy modified action plans if circumstances require a shift in plans and rapid execution of new plans?
<--- Score

90. Is there documentation that will support the successful operation of the improvement?
<--- Score

91. Is there a transfer of ownership and knowledge to process owner and process team tasked with the responsibilities.
<--- Score

92. Does the Chief investment officer performance meet the customer's requirements?
<--- Score

93. Will the team be available to assist members in planning investigations?

<--- Score

94. What other areas of the group might benefit from the Chief investment officer team's improvements, knowledge, and learning?

<--- Score

95. How will the process owner verify improvement in present and future sigma levels, process capabilities?

<--- Score

Add up total points for this section:
_____ = Total points for this section

Divided by: _____ (number of statements answered) = _____ Average score for this section

Transfer your score to the Chief investment officer Index at the beginning of the Self-Assessment.

CRITERION #7: SUSTAIN:

INTENT: Retain the benefits.

In my belief, the answer to this question is clearly defined:

5 Strongly Agree

4 Agree

3 Neutral

2 Disagree

1 Strongly Disagree

1. Which Chief investment officer goals are the most important?
<--- Score

2. How does Chief investment officer integrate with other stakeholder initiatives?
<--- Score

3. What did you miss in the interview for the worst hire you ever made?
<--- Score

4. How will you insure seamless interoperability of Chief investment officer moving forward?
<--- Score

5. What is the overall talent health of your organization as a whole at senior levels, and for each organization reporting to a member of the Senior Leadership Team?
<--- Score

6. Do you think you know, or do you know you know ?
<--- Score

7. What happens if you do not have enough funding?
<--- Score

8. If you got fired and a new hire took your place, what would she do different?
<--- Score

9. Why not do Chief investment officer?
<--- Score

10. Are you maintaining a past–present–future perspective throughout the Chief investment officer discussion?
<--- Score

11. How do you go about securing Chief investment officer?
<--- Score

12. What is the funding source for this project?
<--- Score

13. Do you say no to customers for no reason?
<--- Score

14. Is a Chief investment officer breakthrough on the horizon?
<--- Score

15. Do you see more potential in people than they do in themselves?
<--- Score

16. Are you satisfied with your current role? If not, what is missing from it?
<--- Score

17. What will be the consequences to the stakeholder (financial, reputation etc) if Chief investment officer does not go ahead or fails to deliver the objectives?
<--- Score

18. What counts that you are not counting?
<--- Score

19. Who is responsible for errors?
<--- Score

20. What is your question? Why?
<--- Score

21. How will you ensure you get what you expected?
<--- Score

22. Are all key stakeholders present at all Structured Walkthroughs?
<--- Score

23. How do you foster the skills, knowledge, talents, attributes, and characteristics you want to have?
<--- Score

24. What is the estimated value of the project?
<--- Score

25. Do you have past Chief investment officer successes?
<--- Score

26. What potential megatrends could make your business model obsolete?
<--- Score

27. What role does communication play in the success or failure of a Chief investment officer project?
<--- Score

28. In the past year, what have you done (or could you have done) to increase the accurate perception of your company/brand as ethical and honest?
<--- Score

29. Do you feel that more should be done in the Chief investment officer area?
<--- Score

30. Have new benefits been realized?
<--- Score

31. What Chief investment officer skills are most important?
<--- Score

32. Would you rather sell to knowledgeable and informed customers or to uninformed customers?
<--- Score

33. What is your competitive advantage?
<--- Score

34. What would have to be true for the option on the table to be the best possible choice?
<--- Score

35. How do you make it meaningful in connecting Chief investment officer with what users do day-to-day?
<--- Score

36. When information truly is ubiquitous, when reach and connectivity are completely global, when computing resources are infinite, and when a whole new set of impossibilities are not only possible, but happening, what will that do to your business?
<--- Score

37. How long will it take to change?
<--- Score

38. Who is on the team?
<--- Score

39. What is the overall business strategy?
<--- Score

40. Is the impact that Chief investment officer has shown?
<--- Score

41. What unique value proposition (UVP) do you offer?

<--- Score

42. What are the barriers to increased Chief investment officer production?

<--- Score

43. Whom among your colleagues do you trust, and for what?

<--- Score

44. Who is responsible for Chief investment officer?

<--- Score

45. Why should you adopt a Chief investment officer framework?

<--- Score

46. Do you have the right people on the bus?

<--- Score

47. Who is responsible for ensuring appropriate resources (time, people and money) are allocated to Chief investment officer?

<--- Score

48. What is your BATNA (best alternative to a negotiated agreement)?

<--- Score

49. If you find that you havent accomplished one of the goals for one of the steps of the Chief investment officer strategy, what will you do to fix

it?
<--- Score

50. If you had to leave your organization for a year and the only communication you could have with employees/colleagues was a single paragraph, what would you write?
<--- Score

51. What are the long-term Chief investment officer goals?
<--- Score

52. What you are going to do to affect the numbers?
<--- Score

53. What are strategies for increasing support and reducing opposition?
<--- Score

54. What is an unauthorized commitment?
<--- Score

55. Are you paying enough attention to the partners your company depends on to succeed?
<--- Score

56. How do you track customer value, profitability or financial return, organizational success, and sustainability?
<--- Score

57. Why is Chief investment officer important for you now?
<--- Score

58. How do you deal with Chief investment officer changes?
<--- Score

59. Is your basic point _____ or _____?
<--- Score

60. What goals did you miss?
<--- Score

61. What are the short and long-term Chief investment officer goals?
<--- Score

62. What must you excel at?
<--- Score

63. Where can you break convention?
<--- Score

64. How much does Chief investment officer help?
<--- Score

65. How will you motivate the stakeholders with the least vested interest?
<--- Score

66. Is your strategy driving your strategy? Or is the way in which you allocate resources driving your strategy?
<--- Score

67. What is the range of capabilities?
<--- Score

68. Can you maintain your growth without detracting

from the factors that have contributed to your success?
<--- Score

69. Who do you want your customers to become?
<--- Score

70. How likely is it that a customer would recommend your company to a friend or colleague?
<--- Score

71. What are the potential basics of Chief investment officer fraud?
<--- Score

72. What are you challenging?
<--- Score

73. What are you trying to prove to yourself, and how might it be hijacking your life and business success?
<--- Score

74. How can you negotiate Chief investment officer successfully with a stubborn boss, an irate client, or a deceitful coworker?
<--- Score

75. At what moment would you think; Will I get fired?
<--- Score

76. Do you know what you are doing? And who do you call if you don't?
<--- Score

77. What does your signature ensure?
<--- Score

78. How do you assess the Chief investment officer pitfalls that are inherent in implementing it?
<--- Score

79. Are there any activities that you can take off your to do list?
<--- Score

80. What is the craziest thing you can do?
<--- Score

81. Who else should you help?
<--- Score

82. What is something you believe that nearly no one agrees with you on?
<--- Score

83. Who is the main stakeholder, with ultimate responsibility for driving Chief investment officer forward?
<--- Score

84. What should you stop doing?
<--- Score

85. What trouble can you get into?
<--- Score

86. What one word do you want to own in the minds of your customers, employees, and partners?
<--- Score

87. In retrospect, of the projects that you pulled the plug on, what percent do you wish had been allowed to keep going, and what percent do you wish had ended earlier?
<--- Score

88. What information is critical to your organization that your executives are ignoring?
<--- Score

89. How do you set Chief investment officer stretch targets and how do you get people to not only participate in setting these stretch targets but also that they strive to achieve these?
<--- Score

90. What was the last experiment you ran?
<--- Score

91. Who will provide the final approval of Chief investment officer deliverables?
<--- Score

92. Think of your Chief investment officer project, what are the main functions?
<--- Score

93. What are the essentials of internal Chief investment officer management?
<--- Score

94. Is there any existing Chief investment officer governance structure?
<--- Score

95. What threat is Chief investment officer addressing?

<--- Score

96. How do you manage Chief investment officer Knowledge Management (KM)?
<--- Score

97. Political -is anyone trying to undermine this project?
<--- Score

98. How do you govern and fulfill your societal responsibilities?
<--- Score

99. Are you changing as fast as the world around you?
<--- Score

100. Have benefits been optimized with all key stakeholders?
<--- Score

101. Who will determine interim and final deadlines?
<--- Score

102. What new services of functionality will be implemented next with Chief investment officer ?
<--- Score

103. Are you using a design thinking approach and integrating Innovation, Chief investment officer Experience, and Brand Value?
<--- Score

104. How do you keep the momentum going?
<--- Score

105. How do you ensure that implementations of Chief investment officer products are done in a way that ensures safety?
<--- Score

106. What are the challenges?
<--- Score

107. Is there any reason to believe the opposite of my current belief?
<--- Score

108. Who do we want your customers to become?
<--- Score

109. What happens when a new employee joins the organization?
<--- Score

110. How do you accomplish your long range Chief investment officer goals?
<--- Score

111. How do you engage the workforce, in addition to satisfying them?
<--- Score

112. Who, on the executive team or the board, has spoken to a customer recently?
<--- Score

113. What is the purpose of Chief investment officer in relation to the mission?
<--- Score

114. What would you recommend your friend do if he/

she were facing this dilemma?
<--- Score

115. How do customers see your organization?
<--- Score

116. How will you know that the Chief investment officer project has been successful?
<--- Score

117. Is maximizing Chief investment officer protection the same as minimizing Chief investment officer loss?
<--- Score

118. What trophy do you want on your mantle?
<--- Score

119. What have you done to protect your business from competitive encroachment?
<--- Score

120. Is Chief investment officer realistic, or are you setting yourself up for failure?
<--- Score

121. Will there be any necessary staff changes (redundancies or new hires)?
<--- Score

122. Is a Chief investment officer team work effort in place?
<--- Score

123. How do you create buy-in?
<--- Score

124. What may be the consequences for the performance of an organization if all stakeholders are not consulted regarding Chief investment officer?
<--- Score

125. How do senior leaders deploy your organizations vision and values through your leadership system, to the workforce, to key suppliers and partners, and to customers and other stakeholders, as appropriate?
<--- Score

126. If you were responsible for initiating and implementing major changes in your organization, what steps might you take to ensure acceptance of those changes?
<--- Score

127. What is effective Chief investment officer?
<--- Score

128. Who will manage the integration of tools?
<--- Score

129. Are assumptions made in Chief investment officer stated explicitly?
<--- Score

130. Who are your customers?
<--- Score

131. What have been your experiences in defining long range Chief investment officer goals?
<--- Score

132. What are specific Chief investment officer rules to

follow?

<--- Score

133. What are the business goals Chief investment officer is aiming to achieve?

<--- Score

134. Will it be accepted by users?

<--- Score

135. If you weren't already in this business, would you enter it today? And if not, what are you going to do about it?

<--- Score

136. What are your personal philosophies regarding Chief investment officer and how do they influence your work?

<--- Score

137. How do you know if you are successful?

<--- Score

138. What is the kind of project structure that would be appropriate for your Chief investment officer project, should it be formal and complex, or can it be less formal and relatively simple?

<--- Score

139. Do you have an implicit bias for capital investments over people investments?

<--- Score

140. Is it economical; do you have the time and money?

<--- Score

141. How much contingency will be available in the budget?
<--- Score

142. What do we do when new problems arise?
<--- Score

143. Can you break it down?
<--- Score

144. Can you do all this work?
<--- Score

145. How can you become the company that would put you out of business?
<--- Score

146. Operational - will it work?
<--- Score

147. If there were zero limitations, what would you do differently?
<--- Score

148. What happens at your organization when people fail?
<--- Score

149. Who will be responsible for deciding whether Chief investment officer goes ahead or not after the initial investigations?
<--- Score

150. Are you making progress, and are you making progress as Chief investment officer leaders?

<--- Score

151. Can the schedule be done in the given time?
<--- Score

152. How do you determine the key elements that affect Chief investment officer workforce satisfaction, how are these elements determined for different workforce groups and segments?
<--- Score

153. How do you proactively clarify deliverables and Chief investment officer quality expectations?
<--- Score

154. How do you lead with Chief investment officer in mind?
<--- Score

155. What are your most important goals for the strategic Chief investment officer objectives?
<--- Score

156. In a project to restructure Chief investment officer outcomes, which stakeholders would you involve?
<--- Score

157. What are the rules and assumptions your industry operates under? What if the opposite were true?
<--- Score

158. How do you provide a safe environment -physically and emotionally?
<--- Score

159. How do you keep records, of what?
<--- Score

160. What current systems have to be understood and/or changed?
<--- Score

161. Are new benefits received and understood?
<--- Score

162. Instead of going to current contacts for new ideas, what if you reconnected with dormant contacts--the people you used to know? If you were going reactivate a dormant tie, who would it be?
<--- Score

163. What are the top 3 things at the forefront of your Chief investment officer agendas for the next 3 years?
<--- Score

164. Why should people listen to you?
<--- Score

165. What could happen if you do not do it?
<--- Score

166. What are the success criteria that will indicate that Chief investment officer objectives have been met and the benefits delivered?
<--- Score

167. What are current Chief investment officer paradigms?
<--- Score

168. What projects are going on in the organization today, and what resources are those projects using from the resource pools?

<--- Score

169. Has implementation been effective in reaching specified objectives so far?

<--- Score

170. What management system can you use to leverage the Chief investment officer experience, ideas, and concerns of the people closest to the work to be done?

<--- Score

171. What business benefits will Chief investment officer goals deliver if achieved?

<--- Score

172. How can you become more high-tech but still be high touch?

<--- Score

173. Is Chief investment officer dependent on the successful delivery of a current project?

<--- Score

174. How do you cross-sell and up-sell your Chief investment officer success?

<--- Score

175. Do you have the right capabilities and capacities?

<--- Score

176. If you had to rebuild your organization without any traditional competitive advantages

(i.e., no killer technology, promising research, innovative product/service delivery model, etcetera), how would your people have to approach their work and collaborate together in order to create the necessary conditions for success?

<--- Score

177. Who have you, as a company, historically been when you've been at your best?

<--- Score

178. Were lessons learned captured and communicated?

<--- Score

179. Why do and why don't your customers like your organization?

<--- Score

180. What is the big Chief investment officer idea?

<--- Score

181. How do you transition from the baseline to the target?

<--- Score

182. Are you / should you be revolutionary or evolutionary?

<--- Score

183. Do you think Chief investment officer accomplishes the goals you expect it to accomplish?

<--- Score

184. If your company went out of business tomorrow,

would anyone who doesn't get a paycheck here care?
<--- Score

185. Who uses your product in ways you never expected?

<--- Score

186. How do you listen to customers to obtain actionable information?
<--- Score

187. Do you know who is a friend or a foe?

<--- Score

188. Who are the key stakeholders?

<--- Score

189. Are you relevant? Will you be relevant five years from now? Ten?

<--- Score

190. What knowledge, skills and characteristics mark a good Chief investment officer project manager?
<--- Score

191. Which individuals, teams or departments will be involved in Chief investment officer?
<--- Score

192. What is a feasible sequencing of reform initiatives over time?
<--- Score

193. Marketing budgets are tighter, consumers are more skeptical, and social media has changed forever the way we talk about Chief investment

officer, how do you gain traction?
<--- Score

194. Whose voice (department, ethnic group, women, older workers, etc) might you have missed hearing from in your company, and how might you amplify this voice to create positive momentum for your business?
<--- Score

195. How is implementation research currently incorporated into each of your goals?
<--- Score

196. What is the recommended frequency of auditing?
<--- Score

197. What are the usability implications of Chief investment officer actions?
<--- Score

198. Which models, tools and techniques are necessary?
<--- Score

199. How do you maintain Chief investment officer's Integrity?
<--- Score

200. How are you doing compared to your industry?
<--- Score

201. Is there a work around that you can use?
<--- Score

202. What is it like to work for you?

<--- Score

203. How do you stay inspired?
<--- Score

204. Are your responses positive or negative?
<--- Score

205. What are the key enablers to make this Chief investment officer move?
<--- Score

206. Why will customers want to buy your organizations products/services?
<--- Score

207. What are internal and external Chief investment officer relations?
<--- Score

208. Do Chief investment officer rules make a reasonable demand on a users capabilities?
<--- Score

209. Who do you think the world wants your organization to be?
<--- Score

210. What is your Chief investment officer strategy?
<--- Score

211. What is the source of the strategies for Chief investment officer strengthening and reform?
<--- Score

Add up total points for this section:

_____ = Total points for this section

Divided by: _____ (number of
statements answered) = _____
Average score for this section

Transfer your score to the Chief
investment officer Index at the
beginning of the Self-Assessment.

Chief Investment Officer and Managing Projects, Criteria for Project Managers:

1.0 Initiating Process Group: Chief Investment Officer

1. For technology Chief Investment Officer projects only: Are all production support stakeholders (Business unit, technical support, & user) prepared for implementation with appropriate contingency plans?

2. Contingency planning. if a risk event occurs, what will you do?

3. What do they need to know about the Chief Investment Officer project?

4. Did you use a contractor or vendor?

5. What will you do to minimize the impact should a risk event occur?

6. Have the stakeholders identified all individual requirements pertaining to business process?

7. When must it be done?

8. In which Chief Investment Officer project management process group is the detailed Chief Investment Officer project budget created?

9. Measurable - are the targets measurable?

10. Who supports, improves, and oversees standardized processes related to the Chief Investment Officer projects program?

11. Mitigate. what will you do to minimize the impact

should the risk event occur?

12. Who is behind the Chief Investment Officer project?

13. If the risk event occurs, what will you do?

14. Did the Chief Investment Officer project team have the right skills?

15. The Chief Investment Officer project you are managing has nine stakeholders. How many channel of communications are there between corresponding stakeholders?

16. Who are the Chief Investment Officer project stakeholders?

17. How can you make your needs known?

18. What is the NEXT thing to do?

19. How well did the chosen processes produce the expected results?

20. The Chief Investment Officer project managers have maximum authority in which type of organization?

1.1 Project Charter: Chief Investment Officer

21. Who is the Chief Investment Officer project Manager?

22. What are the assumptions?

23. How much?

24. What goes into your Chief Investment Officer project Charter?

25. What barriers do you predict to your success?

26. Why have you chosen the aim you have set forth?

27. Name and describe the elements that deal with providing the detail?

28. If finished, on what date did it finish?

29. How will you know a change is an improvement?

30. Avoid costs, improve service, and/ or comply with a mandate?

31. What are some examples of a business case?

32. How will you know that a change is an improvement?

33. Why do you manage integration?

34. Major high-level milestone targets: what events measure progress?

35. Pop quiz – which are the same inputs as in the Chief Investment Officer project charter?

36. What are the known stakeholder requirements?

37. Fit with other Products Compliments – Cannibalizes?

38. Does the Chief Investment Officer project need to consider any special capacity or capability issues?

39. Are there special technology requirements?

1.2 Stakeholder Register: Chief Investment Officer

40. Who wants to talk about Security?

41. How will reports be created?

42. Who is managing stakeholder engagement?

43. How much influence do they have on the Chief Investment Officer project?

44. How big is the gap?

45. How should employers make voices heard?

46. What & Why?

47. Who are the stakeholders?

48. Is your organization ready for change?

49. What are the major Chief Investment Officer project milestones requiring communications or providing communications opportunities?

50. What is the power of the stakeholder?

51. What opportunities exist to provide communications?

1.3 Stakeholder Analysis Matrix: Chief Investment Officer

52. How can you counter negative efforts?

53. Who will be responsible for managing the outcome?

54. Political effects?

55. Accreditations, qualifications, certifications?

56. Lack of competitive strength?

57. Contributions to policy and practice?

58. What makes a person a stakeholder?

59. What is the range you need to look at?

60. Tactics: eg, surprise, major contracts?

61. How to measure the achievement of the Outputs?

62. Resource providers; who can provide resources to ensure the implementation of the Chief Investment Officer project?

63. Would it be fair to say that cost is a controlling criteria?

64. Vital contracts and partners?

65. Seasonality, weather effects?

66. If you can not fix it, how do you do it differently?

67. What is the relationship among stakeholders?

68. New technologies, services, ideas?

69. What is in it for you?

70. Who will be affected by the work?

71. How to measure the achievement of the Development Objective?

2.0 Planning Process Group: Chief Investment Officer

72. First of all, should any action be taken?

73. You are creating your WBS and find that you keep decomposing tasks into smaller and smaller units. How can you tell when you are done?

74. What business situation is being addressed?

75. What is a Software Development Life Cycle (SDLC)?

76. Are the necessary foundations in place to ensure the sustainability of the results of the Chief Investment Officer project?

77. How will users learn how to use the deliverables?

78. Have more efficient (sensitive) and appropriate measures been adopted to respond to the political and socio-cultural problems identified?

79. How will it affect you?

80. How should needs be met?

81. Do the partners have sufficient financial capacity to keep up the benefits produced by the programme?

82. What is involved in Chief Investment Officer project scope management, and why is good Chief Investment Officer project scope management

so important on information technology Chief Investment Officer projects?

83. Is the Chief Investment Officer project supported by national and/or local organizations?

84. When will the Chief Investment Officer project be done?

85. To what extent are the participating departments coordinating with each other?

86. Product breakdown structure (pbs): what is the Chief Investment Officer project result or product, and how should it look like, what are its parts?

87. Are you just doing busywork to pass the time?

88. How are it Chief Investment Officer projects different?

89. Just how important is your work to the overall success of the Chief Investment Officer project?

90. How well do the team follow the chosen processes?

2.1 Project Management Plan: Chief Investment Officer

91. What are the deliverables?

92. What are the training needs?

93. Are calculations and results of analyzes essentially correct?

94. What should you drop in order to add something new?

95. Does the selected plan protect privacy?

96. What data/reports/tools/etc. do your PMs need?

97. What is risk management?

98. Who is the sponsor?

99. Are there any windfall benefits that would accrue to the Chief Investment Officer project sponsor or other parties?

100. How do you organize the costs in the Chief Investment Officer project management plan?

101. Is the budget realistic?

102. Why Change?

103. How do you manage time?

104. Are there any client staffing expectations?

105. Do there need to be organizational changes?

106. Are there non-structural buyout or relocation recommendations?

107. What happened during the process that you found interesting?

108. What worked well?

2.2 Scope Management Plan: Chief Investment Officer

109. Has the Chief Investment Officer project scope been baselined?

110. Are the results of quality assurance reviews provided to affected groups & individuals?

111. Are actuals compared against estimates to analyze and correct variances?

112. Are vendor contract reports, reviews and visits conducted periodically?

113. Are stakeholders aware and supportive of the principles and practices of modern software estimation?

114. Is there a formal set of procedures supporting Stakeholder Management?

115. Are milestone deliverables effectively tracked and compared to Chief Investment Officer project plan?

116. How do you know how you are doing?

117. Is there a formal process for updating the Chief Investment Officer project baseline?

118. Is your organization structure for both tracking & controlling the budget well defined and assigned to a

specific individual?

119. Are the budget estimates reasonable?

120. Is there a Chief Investment Officer project organization chart showing the reporting relationships and responsibilities for each position?

121. To whom will the deliverables be first presented for inspection and verification?

122. Are all payments made according to the contract(s)?

123. Product – what are you trying to accomplish and how will you know when you are finished?

124. Pop quiz – what changed on Chief Investment Officer project scope statement input?

125. Knowing the health of the Chief Investment Officer project – What is the status?

126. What are the risks that could significantly affect the communication on the Chief Investment Officer project?

127. Are the proposed Chief Investment Officer project purposes different than the previously authorized Chief Investment Officer project?

2.3 Requirements Management Plan: Chief Investment Officer

128. When and how will a requirements baseline be established in this Chief Investment Officer project?

129. Did you get proper approvals?

130. Will you have access to stakeholders when you need them?

131. Is there formal agreement on who has authority to approve a change in requirements?

132. Will you use tracing to help understand the impact of a change in requirements?

133. Did you use declarative statements?

134. Controlling Chief Investment Officer project requirements involves monitoring the status of the Chief Investment Officer project requirements and managing changes to the requirements. Who is responsible for monitoring and tracking the Chief Investment Officer project requirements?

135. Will you use an assessment of the Chief Investment Officer project environment as a tool to discover risk to the requirements process?

136. How will bidders price evaluations be done, by deliverables, phases, or in a big bang?

137. Who will do the reporting and to whom will reports be delivered?

138. What are you counting on?

139. Do you have an appropriate arrangement for meetings?

140. How do you know that you have done this right?

141. What went wrong?

142. What is the earliest finish date for this Chief Investment Officer project if it is scheduled to start on ...?

143. Is there formal agreement on who has authority to request a change in requirements?

144. Will the Chief Investment Officer project requirements become approved in writing?

145. Who is responsible for quantifying the Chief Investment Officer project requirements?

146. Should you include sub-activities?

147. The wbs is developed as part of a joint planning session. and how do you know that youhave done this right?

2.4 Requirements Documentation: Chief Investment Officer

148. Who is interacting with the system?

149. How does the proposed Chief Investment Officer project contribute to the overall objectives of your organization?

150. Is the origin of the requirement clearly stated?

151. If applicable; are there issues linked with the fact that this is an offshore Chief Investment Officer project?

152. What if the system wasn t implemented?

153. Where do you define what is a customer, what are the attributes of customer?

154. Is your business case still valid?

155. Is new technology needed?

156. Does the system provide the functions which best support the customers needs?

157. Who is involved?

158. Are all functions required by the customer included?

159. What is a show stopper in the requirements?

160. Are there legal issues?

161. What is the risk associated with the technology?

162. How do you know when a Requirement is accurate enough?

163. Can you check system requirements?

164. What are the attributes of a customer?

165. How linear / iterative is your Requirements Gathering process (or will it be)?

166. What can tools do for us?

167. Where do system and software requirements come from, what are sources?

2.5 Requirements Traceability Matrix: Chief Investment Officer

168. Is there a requirements traceability process in place?

169. How will it affect the stakeholders personally in career?

170. What are the chronologies, contingencies, consequences, criteria?

171. How do you manage scope?

172. Will you use a Requirements Traceability Matrix?

173. How small is small enough?

174. Do you have a clear understanding of all subcontracts in place?

175. What percentage of Chief Investment Officer projects are producing traceability matrices between requirements and other work products?

176. What is the WBS?

177. Describe the process for approving requirements so they can be added to the traceability matrix and Chief Investment Officer project work can be performed. Will the Chief Investment Officer project requirements become approved in writing?

178. Why use a WBS?

179. Why do you manage scope?

2.6 Project Scope Statement: Chief Investment Officer

180. Was planning completed before the Chief Investment Officer project was initiated?

181. Have you been able to thoroughly document the Chief Investment Officer projects assumptions and constraints?

182. Is the Chief Investment Officer project sponsor function identified and defined?

183. Which risks does the Chief Investment Officer project focus on?

184. What process would you recommend for creating the Chief Investment Officer project scope statement?

185. Will the risk status be reported to management on a regular and frequent basis?

186. Will the risk documents be filed?

187. Are the meetings set up to have assigned note takers that will add action/issues to the issue list?

188. Is there a Quality Assurance Plan documented and filed?

189. Is the Chief Investment Officer project manager qualified and experienced in Chief Investment Officer project management?

190. Are there completion/verification criteria defined for each task producing an output?

191. Were potential customers involved early in the planning process?

192. Are there backup strategies for key members of the Chief Investment Officer project?

193. If the scope changes, what will the impact be to your Chief Investment Officer project in terms of duration, cost, quality, or any other important areas of the Chief Investment Officer project?

194. Have the reports to be produced, distributed, and filed been defined?

195. Will there be a Change Control Process in place?

196. Are there adequate Chief Investment Officer project control systems?

197. Will the Chief Investment Officer project risks be managed according to the Chief Investment Officer projects risk management process?

198. What are the major deliverables of the Chief Investment Officer project?

199. Is there a Change Management Board?

2.7 Assumption and Constraint Log: Chief Investment Officer

200. Would known impacts serve as impediments?

201. Have all necessary approvals been obtained?

202. Do documented requirements exist for all critical components and areas, including technical, business, interfaces, performance, security and conversion requirements?

203. How many Chief Investment Officer project staff does this specific process affect?

204. Do the requirements meet the standards of correctness, completeness, consistency, accuracy, and readability?

205. Have all involved stakeholders and work groups committed to the Chief Investment Officer project?

206. Has a Chief Investment Officer project Communications Plan been developed?

207. Is the process working, and people are not executing in compliance of the process?

208. If appropriate, is the deliverable content consistent with current Chief Investment Officer project documents and in compliance with the Document Management Plan?

209. Does a specific action and/or state that is known to violate security policy occur?

210. Does the system design reflect the requirements?

211. Does the Chief Investment Officer project have a formal Chief Investment Officer project Plan?

212. How are new requirements or changes to requirements identified?

213. If it is out of compliance, should the process be amended or should the Plan be amended?

214. Is the current scope of the Chief Investment Officer project substantially different than that originally defined in the approved Chief Investment Officer project plan?

215. What strengths do you have?

216. What if failure during recovery?

217. What other teams / processes would be impacted by changes to the current process, and how?

2.8 Work Breakdown Structure: Chief Investment Officer

218. What is the probability that the Chief Investment Officer project duration will exceed xx weeks?

219. Why would you develop a Work Breakdown Structure?

220. Can you make it?

221. Is it a change in scope?

222. Do you need another level?

223. Who has to do it?

224. How big is a work-package?

225. What is the probability of completing the Chief Investment Officer project in less that xx days?

226. When do you stop?

227. How far down?

228. When does it have to be done?

229. Where does it take place?

230. How will you and your Chief Investment Officer project team define the Chief Investment Officer projects scope and work breakdown structure?

231. What has to be done?

232. Why is it useful?

2.9 WBS Dictionary: Chief Investment Officer

233. Are Chief Investment Officer projected overhead costs in each pool and the associated direct costs used as the basis for establishing interim rates for allocating overhead to contracts?

234. Is undistributed budget limited to contract effort which cannot yet be planned to CWBS elements at or below the level specified for reporting to the Government?

235. Is the anticipated (firm and potential) business base Chief Investment Officer projected in a rational, consistent manner?

236. Contemplated overhead expenditure for each period based on the best information currently available?

237. Is each control account assigned to a single organizational element directly responsible for the work and identifiable to a single element of the CWBS?

238. Are the bases and rates for allocating costs from each indirect pool to commercial work consistent with the already stated used to allocate corresponding costs to Government contracts?

239. Appropriate work authorization documents which subdivide the contractual effort and

responsibilities, within functional organizations?

240. Changes in the overhead pool and/or organization structures?

241. Are the wbs and organizational levels for application of the Chief Investment Officer projected overhead costs identified?

242. Are data elements (BCWS, BCWP, and ACWP) progressively summarized from the detail level to the contract level through the CWBS?

243. Authorization to proceed with all authorized work?

244. Software specification, development, integration, and testing, licenses ?

245. Does the contractor require sufficient detailed planning of control accounts to constrain the application of budget initially allocated for future effort to current effort?

246. Are records maintained to show full accountability for all material purchased for the contract, including the residual inventory?

247. Are procedures established to prevent changes to the contract budget base other than the already stated authorized by contractual action?

248. Are current work performance indicators and goals relatable to original goals as modified by contractual changes, replanning, and reprogramming actions?

249. Are management actions taken to reduce indirect costs when there are significant adverse variances?

250. Does the contractors system provide unit costs, equivalent unit or lot costs in terms of labor, material, other direct, and indirect costs?

2.10 Schedule Management Plan: Chief Investment Officer

251. What will be the final cost of the Chief Investment Officer project if status quo is maintained?

252. Is the correct WBS element identified for each task and milestone in the IMS?

253. Are adequate resources provided for the quality assurance function?

254. Are internal Chief Investment Officer project status meetings held at reasonable intervals?

255. What tools and techniques will be used to estimate activity durations?

256. Are estimating assumptions and constraints captured?

257. Will the tools selected accomplish the scheduling needs?

258. Are Chief Investment Officer project team members committed fulltime?

259. Have external dependencies been captured in the schedule?

260. Is there an approved case?

261. Has the Chief Investment Officer project manager

been identified?

262. Are all vendor contracts closed out?

263. Are decisions captured in a decisions log?

264. Are mitigation strategies identified?

265. Has a quality assurance plan been developed for the Chief Investment Officer project?

266. Are procurement deliverables arriving on time and to specification?

267. Are the activity durations realistic and at an appropriate level of detail for effective management?

268. Are all key components of a Quality Assurance Plan present?

269. Have reserves been created to address risks?

270. Is funded schedule margin reasonable and logically distributed?

2.11 Activity List: Chief Investment Officer

271. What is the LF and LS for each activity?

272. Are the required resources available or need to be acquired?

273. Where will it be performed?

274. Is infrastructure setup part of your Chief Investment Officer project?

275. How do you determine the late start (LS) for each activity?

276. For other activities, how much delay can be tolerated?

277. How much slack is available in the Chief Investment Officer project?

278. How will it be performed?

279. When will the work be performed?

280. Is there anything planned that does not need to be here?

281. How can the Chief Investment Officer project be displayed graphically to better visualize the activities?

282. What is your organizations history in doing

similar activities?

283. What is the probability the Chief Investment Officer project can be completed in xx weeks?

284. How should ongoing costs be monitored to try to keep the Chief Investment Officer project within budget?

285. What went well?

286. Who will perform the work?

287. When do the individual activities need to start and finish?

288. Can you determine the activity that must finish, before this activity can start?

2.12 Activity Attributes: Chief Investment Officer

289. What is the general pattern here?

290. Where else does it apply?

291. Is there a trend during the year?

292. Have constraints been applied to the start and finish milestones for the phases?

293. How much activity detail is required?

294. How else could the items be grouped?

295. Are the required resources available?

296. What is missing?

297. Why?

298. Resource is assigned to?

299. Were there other ways you could have organized the data to achieve similar results?

300. Can you re-assign any activities to another resource to resolve an over-allocation?

301. How difficult will it be to do specific activities on this Chief Investment Officer project?

302. What activity do you think you should spend the most time on?

303. Resources to accomplish the work?

304. Which method produces the more accurate cost assignment?

305. Can more resources be added?

2.13 Milestone List: Chief Investment Officer

306. Calculate how long can activity be delayed?

307. Global influences?

308. Legislative effects?

309. Sustaining internal capabilities?

310. Describe the industry you are in and the market growth opportunities. What is the market for your technology, product or service?

311. It is to be a narrative text providing the crucial aspects of your Chief Investment Officer project proposal answering what, who, how, when and where?

312. Sustainable financial backing?

313. Continuity, supply chain robustness?

314. What has been done so far?

315. Describe your organizations strengths and core competencies. What factors will make your organization succeed?

316. How difficult will it be to do specific activities on this Chief Investment Officer project?

317. Usps (unique selling points)?

318. How soon can the activity finish?

319. Level of the Innovation?

320. Identify critical paths (one or more) and which activities are on the critical path?

321. Insurmountable weaknesses?

322. When will the Chief Investment Officer project be complete?

2.14 Network Diagram: Chief Investment Officer

323. How confident can you be in your milestone dates and the delivery date?

324. What activities must occur simultaneously with this activity?

325. Exercise: what is the probability that the Chief Investment Officer project duration will exceed xx weeks?

326. If x is long, what would be the completion time if you break x into two parallel parts of y weeks and z weeks?

327. What activities must follow this activity?

328. What is the probability of completing the Chief Investment Officer project in less that xx days?

329. Are you on time?

330. What are the Major Administrative Issues?

331. What controls the start and finish of a job?

332. What are the tools?

333. What job or jobs precede it?

334. What job or jobs could run concurrently?

335. What activity must be completed immediately before this activity can start?

336. What to do and When?

337. What can be done concurrently?

338. Planning: who, how long, what to do?

339. Where do you schedule uncertainty time?

2.15 Activity Resource Requirements: Chief Investment Officer

340. Do you use tools like decomposition and rolling-wave planning to produce the activity list and other outputs?

341. What are constraints that you might find during the Human Resource Planning process?

342. When does monitoring begin?

343. Time for overtime?

344. Are there unresolved issues that need to be addressed?

345. Other support in specific areas?

346. Anything else?

347. How do you handle petty cash?

348. Why do you do that?

349. How many signatures do you require on a check and does this match what is in your policy and procedures?

350. Organizational Applicability?

351. What is the Work Plan Standard?

352. Which logical relationship does the PDM use most often?

2.16 Resource Breakdown Structure: Chief Investment Officer

353. Who delivers the information?

354. Changes based on input from stakeholders?

355. Who is allowed to see what data about which resources?

356. How difficult will it be to do specific activities on this Chief Investment Officer project?

357. Goals for the Chief Investment Officer project. What is each stakeholders desired outcome for the Chief Investment Officer project?

358. What is the purpose of assigning and documenting responsibility?

359. Who needs what information?

360. Which resources should be in the resource pool?

361. What is the number one predictor of a groups productivity?

362. What is the difference between % Complete and % work?

363. Any changes from stakeholders?

364. How should the information be delivered?

365. What is Chief Investment Officer project communication management?

366. Why is this important?

367. Who is allowed to perform which functions?

368. The list could probably go on, but, the thing that you would most like to know is, How long & How much?

369. Is predictive resource analysis being done?

370. What is each stakeholders desired outcome for the Chief Investment Officer project?

2.17 Activity Duration Estimates: Chief Investment Officer

371. Does a process exist to identify Chief Investment Officer project roles, responsibilities and reporting relationships?

372. Are risks that are likely to affect the Chief Investment Officer project identified and documented?

373. Will it help promote wellness at your organization and reduce insurance costs?

374. Do you agree with the suggestions provided for improving Chief Investment Officer project communications?

375. Is the work performed reviewed against contractual objectives?

376. Are expert judgment and historical information utilized to estimate activity duration?

377. What are key inputs and outputs of the software?

378. How much time is required to develop it?

379. Briefly summarize the work done by Maslow, Herzberg, McClellan, McGregor, Ouchi, Thamhain and Wilemon, and Covey. How do theories relate to Chief Investment Officer project management?

380. Which includes asking team members about the time estimates for activities and reaching agreement on the calendar date for each activity?

381. What is the shortest possible time it will take to complete this Chief Investment Officer project?

382. Which tips for taking the PMP exam do you think would be most helpful for you?

383. Which types of reports would help provide summary information to senior management?

384. Based on , if you need to shorten the duration of the Chief Investment Officer project, what activity would you try to shorten?

385. What functions does this software provide that cannot be done easily using other tools such as a spreadsheet or database?

386. Who will be the main sponsor for it?

387. What are some crucial elements of a good Chief Investment Officer project plan?

388. Calculate the expected duration for an activity that has a most likely time of 3, a pessimistic time of 10, and a optimiztic time of 2?

389. Why do you think schedule issues often cause the most conflicts on Chief Investment Officer projects?

2.18 Duration Estimating Worksheet: Chief Investment Officer

390. What went right?

391. Why estimate costs?

392. Can the Chief Investment Officer project be constructed as planned?

393. What is your role?

394. Small or large Chief Investment Officer project?

395. Value pocket identification & quantification what are value pockets?

396. Do any colleagues have experience with your organization and/or RFPs?

397. What utility impacts are there?

398. Is a construction detail attached (to aid in explanation)?

399. Is this operation cost effective?

400. Is the Chief Investment Officer project responsive to community need?

401. What is an Average Chief Investment Officer project?

402. What questions do you have?

403. Will the Chief Investment Officer project collaborate with the local community and leverage resources?

404. Why estimate time and cost?

405. How should ongoing costs be monitored to try to keep the Chief Investment Officer project within budget?

406. What is the total time required to complete the Chief Investment Officer project if no delays occur?

407. What info is needed?

2.19 Project Schedule: Chief Investment Officer

408. Understand the constraints used in preparing the schedule. Are activities connected because logic dictates the order in which others occur?

409. How effectively were issues able to be resolved without impacting the Chief Investment Officer project Schedule or Budget?

410. What documents, if any, will the subcontractor provide (eg Chief Investment Officer project schedule, quality plan etc)?

411. Why do you need to manage Chief Investment Officer project Risk?

412. To what degree is do you feel the entire team was committed to the Chief Investment Officer project schedule?

413. Month Chief Investment Officer project take?

414. Your best shot for providing estimations how complex/how much work does the activity require?

415. Why do you think schedule issues often cause the most conflicts on Chief Investment Officer projects?

416. How closely did the initial Chief Investment Officer project Schedule compare with the actual schedule?

417. Activity charts and bar charts are graphical representations of a Chief Investment Officer project schedule ...how do they differ?

418. Verify that the update is accurate. Are all remaining durations correct?

419. Your Chief Investment Officer project management plan results in a Chief Investment Officer project schedule that is too long. If the Chief Investment Officer project network diagram cannot change and you have extra personnel resources, what is the BEST thing to do?

420. What is the difference?

421. Are procedures defined by which the Chief Investment Officer project schedule may be changed?

422. How does a Chief Investment Officer project get to be a year late ?

423. Is the Chief Investment Officer project schedule available for all Chief Investment Officer project team members to review?

424. It allows the Chief Investment Officer project to be delivered on schedule. How Do you Use Schedules?

425. Are there activities that came from a template or previous Chief Investment Officer project that are not applicable on this phase of this Chief Investment Officer project?

426. What is Chief Investment Officer project management?

2.20 Cost Management Plan: Chief Investment Officer

427. Does the schedule include Chief Investment Officer project management time and change request analysis time?

428. Cost estimate preparation – What cost estimates will be prepared during the Chief Investment Officer project phases?

429. Are risk oriented checklists used during risk identification?

430. Does a documented Chief Investment Officer project organizational policy & plan (i.e. governance model) exist?

431. Are meeting minutes captured and sent out after the meeting?

432. Timeline and milestones?

433. Pareto diagrams, statistical sampling, flow charting or trend analysis used quality monitoring?

434. Has the scope management document been updated and distributed to help prevent scope creep?

435. Is there a requirements change management processes in place?

436. Has a sponsor been identified?

437. Chief Investment Officer project Objectives?

438. What is the work breakdown structure for the Chief Investment Officer project?

439. Is current scope of the Chief Investment Officer project substantially different than that originally defined?

440. Do Chief Investment Officer project managers participating in the Chief Investment Officer project know the Chief Investment Officer projects true status first hand?

441. Have the reasons why the changes to your organizational systems and capabilities are required?

442. Exclusions – is there scope to be performed or provided by others?

443. Are issues raised, assessed, actioned, and resolved in a timely and efficient manner?

2.21 Activity Cost Estimates: Chief Investment Officer

444. What is Chief Investment Officer project cost management?

445. What makes a good expected result statement?

446. Does the activity serve a common type of customer?

447. Does the activity use a common approach or business function to deliver its results?

448. How do you fund change orders?

449. How many activities should you have?

450. Would you hire them again?

451. How do you change activities?

452. Padding is bad and contingencies are good. what is the difference?

453. Specific - is the objective clear in terms of what, how, when, and where the situation will be changed?

454. Can you delete activities or make them inactive?

455. Eac -estimate at completion, what is the total job expected to cost?

456. What is a Chief Investment Officer project Management Plan?

457. Were escalated issues resolved promptly?

458. What is the activity inventory?

459. How difficult will it be to do specific tasks on the Chief Investment Officer project?

460. What communication items need improvement?

461. Are data needed on characteristics of care?

462. How and when do you enter into Chief Investment Officer project Procurement Management?

2.22 Cost Estimating Worksheet: Chief Investment Officer

463. What additional Chief Investment Officer project(s) could be initiated as a result of this Chief Investment Officer project?

464. What can be included?

465. Ask: are others positioned to know, are others credible, and will others cooperate?

466. What is the purpose of estimating?

467. Is it feasible to establish a control group arrangement?

468. What is the estimated labor cost today based upon this information?

469. Will the Chief Investment Officer project collaborate with the local community and leverage resources?

470. Can a trend be established from historical performance data on the selected measure and are the criteria for using trend analysis or forecasting methods met?

471. Identify the timeframe necessary to monitor progress and collect data to determine how the selected measure has changed?

472. What costs are to be estimated?

473. Who is best positioned to know and assist in identifying corresponding factors?

474. How will the results be shared and to whom?

475. Is the Chief Investment Officer project responsive to community need?

476. What will others want?

477. Does the Chief Investment Officer project provide innovative ways for stakeholders to overcome obstacles or deliver better outcomes?

478. What happens to any remaining funds not used?

2.23 Cost Baseline: Chief Investment Officer

479. Has the actual cost of the Chief Investment Officer project (or Chief Investment Officer project phase) been tallied and compared to the approved budget?

480. Does the suggested change request seem to represent a necessary enhancement to the product?

481. Are procedures defined by which the cost baseline may be changed?

482. Review your risk triggers -have your risks changed?

483. At which frequency ?

484. Are you meeting with your team regularly?

485. Has training and knowledge transfer of the operations organization been completed?

486. What is the reality?

487. How difficult will it be to do specific tasks on the Chief Investment Officer project?

488. How fast?

489. How will cost estimates be used?

490. What is the consequence?

491. If you sold 10x widgets on a day, what would the affect on profits be?

492. What does a good WBS NOT look like?

493. Has the Chief Investment Officer project documentation been archived or otherwise disposed as described in the Chief Investment Officer project communication plan?

494. Have you identified skills that are missing from your team?

495. Have all approved changes to the cost baseline been identified and impact on the Chief Investment Officer project documented?

496. Does the suggested change request represent a desired enhancement to the products functionality?

497. What weaknesses do you have?

2.24 Quality Management Plan: Chief Investment Officer

498. Does the plan conform to standards?

499. How are changes recorded?

500. Is there a procedure for this process?

501. How are people conducting sampling trained?

502. How are records kept in the office?

503. How relevant is this attribute to this Chief Investment Officer project or audit?

504. Contradictory information between document sections?

505. How does your organization measure customer satisfaction/dissatisfaction?

506. How is staff trained in procedures?

507. Are qmps good forever?

508. Who do you send data to?

509. Is there a Quality Management Plan?

510. Has a Chief Investment Officer project Communications Plan been developed?

511. How do you decide who is responsible for signing the data reports?

512. Are there unnecessary steps that are creating bottlenecks and/or causing people to wait?

513. Are requirements management tracking tools and procedures in place?

514. What is quality planning ?

515. When reporting to different audiences, do you vary the form or type of report?

516. How do you check in-coming sample material?

517. What changes can you make that will result in improvement?

2.25 Quality Metrics: Chief Investment Officer

518. What if the biggest risk to your business were the already stated people who do not complain?

519. What method of measurement do you use?

520. What are you trying to accomplish?

521. What are your organizations expectations for its quality Chief Investment Officer project?

522. Are interface issues coordinated?

523. Do you stratify metrics by product or site?

524. What is the CMS Benchmark?

525. How does one achieve stability?

526. Which report did you use to create the data you are submitting?

527. Was review conducted per standard protocols?

528. When is the security analysis testing complete?

529. Are documents on hand to provide explanations of privacy and confidentiality?

530. How do you calculate such metrics?

531. What group is empowered to define quality requirements?

532. Is the reporting frequency appropriate?

533. Do you know how much profit a 10% decrease in waste would generate?

534. Is quality culture a competitive advantage?

535. How exactly do you define when differences exist?

536. Why is now the time for quality metrics?

2.26 Process Improvement Plan: Chief Investment Officer

537. Where do you want to be?

538. What is quality and how will you ensure it?

539. What personnel are the champions for the initiative?

540. What actions are needed to address the problems and achieve the goals?

541. What is the test-cycle concept?

542. How do you manage quality?

543. How do you measure?

544. Everyone agrees on what process improvement is, right?

545. Does your process ensure quality?

546. The motive is determined by asking, Why do you want to achieve this goal?

547. What personnel are the sponsors for that initiative?

548. If a process improvement framework is being used, which elements will help the problems and goals listed?

549. Where are you now?

550. Management commitment at all levels?

551. Does explicit definition of the measures exist?

552. Are there forms and procedures to collect and record the data?

553. Are you making progress on your improvement plan?

554. Are you meeting the quality standards?

555. Modeling current processes is great, and will you ever see a return on that investment?

556. Have storage and access mechanisms and procedures been determined?

2.27 Responsibility Assignment Matrix: Chief Investment Officer

557. Too many rs: with too many people labeled as doing the work, are there too many hands involved?

558. Direct labor dollars and/or hours?

559. The anticipated business volume?

560. Are indirect costs accumulated for comparison with the corresponding budgets?

561. How do you assist them to be as productive as possible?

562. Does the contractor use objective results, design reviews, and tests to trace schedule?

563. Budgeted cost for work performed?

564. What can you do to improve productivity?

565. Are control accounts opened and closed based on the start and completion of work contained therein?

566. Will too many Communicating responsibilities tangle the Chief Investment Officer project in unnecessary communications?

567. Competencies and craftsmanship – what competencies are necessary and what level?

568. How do you manage human resources?

569. Does the scheduling system identify in a timely manner the status of work?

570. Is the entire contract planned in time-phased control accounts to the extent practicable?

571. Budgets assigned to major functional organizations?

572. What travel needed?

573. Are there any drawbacks to using a responsibility assignment matrix?

574. Is work properly classified as measured effort, LOE, or apportioned effort and appropriately separated?

2.28 Roles and Responsibilities: Chief Investment Officer

575. What is working well within your organizations performance management system?

576. Required skills, knowledge, experience?

577. What should you do now to prepare yourself for a promotion, increased responsibilities or a different job?

578. Be specific; avoid generalities. Thank you and great work alone are insufficient. What exactly do you appreciate and why?

579. Was the expectation clearly communicated?

580. What should you do now to ensure that you are meeting all expectations of your current position?

581. Does the team have access to and ability to use data analysis tools?

582. Implementation of actions: Who are the responsible units?

583. Are your policies supportive of a culture of quality data?

584. Once the responsibilities are defined for the Chief Investment Officer project, have the deliverables, roles and responsibilities been clearly communicated

to every participant?

585. How is your work-life balance?

586. What specific behaviors did you observe?

587. Have you ever been a part of this team?

588. Attainable / achievable: the goal is attainable; can you actually accomplish the goal?

589. Who is responsible for implementation activities and where will the functions, roles and responsibilities be defined?

590. Influence: what areas of organizational decision making are you able to influence when you do not have authority to make the final decision?

591. Do the values and practices inherent in the culture of your organization foster or hinder the process?

592. Are governance roles and responsibilities documented?

593. Where are you most strong as a supervisor?

2.29 Human Resource Management Plan: Chief Investment Officer

594. Is the assigned Chief Investment Officer project manager a PMP (Certified Chief Investment Officer project manager) and experienced?

595. Is the Chief Investment Officer project sponsor clearly communicating the business case or rationale for why this Chief Investment Officer project is needed?

596. Were the budget estimates reasonable?

597. Has your organization readiness assessment been conducted?

598. Do all stakeholders know how to access this repository and where to find the Chief Investment Officer project documentation?

599. What skills, knowledge and experiences are required?

600. Are software metrics formally captured, analyzed and used as a basis for other Chief Investment Officer project estimates?

601. Are trade-offs between accepting the risk and mitigating the risk identified?

602. Chief Investment Officer project definition & scope?

603. Is current scope of the Chief Investment Officer project substantially different than that originally defined?

604. Is there an onboarding process in place?

605. Has a provision been made to reassess Chief Investment Officer project risks at various Chief Investment Officer project stages?

606. Have the procedures for identifying budget variances been followed?

607. How complete is the human resource management plan?

608. Has a capability assessment been conducted?

609. Do you have the reasons why the changes to your organizational systems and capabilities are required?

610. Were Chief Investment Officer project team members involved in detailed estimating and scheduling?

611. Has a quality assurance plan been developed for the Chief Investment Officer project?

612. Are the quality tools and methods identified in the Quality Plan appropriate to the Chief Investment Officer project?

613. What were things that you did very well and want to do the same again on the next Chief Investment

Officer project?

2.30 Communications Management Plan: Chief Investment Officer

614. What data is going to be required?

615. What is the stakeholders level of authority?

616. How will the person responsible for executing the communication item be notified?

617. Timing: when do the effects of the communication take place?

618. Why do you manage communications?

619. How did the term stakeholder originate?

620. How often do you engage with stakeholders?

621. Who to learn from?

622. Are you constantly rushing from meeting to meeting?

623. Are there potential barriers between the team and the stakeholder?

624. What is Chief Investment Officer project communications management?

625. Which stakeholders can influence others?

626. Who have you worked with in past, similar

initiatives?

627. What help do you and your team need from the stakeholder?

628. Is the stakeholder role recognized by your organization?

629. Do you then often overlook a key stakeholder or stakeholder group?

630. Who will use or be affected by the result of a Chief Investment Officer project?

631. Which stakeholders are thought leaders, influences, or early adopters?

632. What approaches do you use?

633. Can you think of other people who might have concerns or interests?

2.31 Risk Management Plan: Chief Investment Officer

634. Anticipated volatility of the requirements?

635. Monitoring -what factors can you track that will enable you to determine if the risk is becoming more or less likely?

636. Mitigation -how can you avoid the risk?

637. Should the risk be taken at all?

638. Is the customer willing to participate in reviews?

639. How would you suggest monitoring for risk transition indicators?

640. Technology risk: is the Chief Investment Officer project technically feasible?

641. What will the damage be?

642. Can the risk be avoided by choosing a different alternative?

643. Is this an issue, action item, question or a risk?

644. Costs associated with late delivery or a defective product?

645. What did not work so well?

646. How will the Chief Investment Officer project know if your organizations risk response actions were effective?

647. Does the customer have a solid idea of what is required?

648. How quickly does each item need to be resolved?

649. Are the participants able to keep up with the workload?

650. Management -what contingency plans do you have if the risk becomes a reality?

651. Is Chief Investment Officer project scope stable?

652. What is the impact to the Chief Investment Officer project if the item is not resolved in a timely fashion?

2.32 Risk Register: Chief Investment Officer

653. What action, if any, has been taken to respond to the risk?

654. Are implemented controls working as others should?

655. Amongst the action plans and recommendations that you have to introduce are there some that could stop or delay the overall program?

656. Having taken action, how did the responses effect change, and where is the Chief Investment Officer project now?

657. What are the major risks facing the Chief Investment Officer project?

658. Have other controls and solutions been implemented in other services which could be applied as an alternative to additional funding?

659. Assume the event happens, what is the Most Likely impact?

660. Manageability – have mitigations to the risk been identified?

661. Are corrective measures implemented as planned?

662. How is a Community Risk Register created?

663. Risk probability and impact: how will the probabilities and impacts of risk items be assessed?

664. Why would you develop a risk register?

665. Assume the risk event or situation happens, what would the impact be?

666. What should you do now?

667. What is the probability and impact of the risk occurring?

668. What are your key risks/show istoppers and what is being done to manage them?

669. Preventative actions - planned actions to reduce the likelihood a risk will occur and/or reduce the seriousness should it occur. What should you do now?

670. People risk -are people with appropriate skills available to help complete the Chief Investment Officer project?

671. Does the evidence highlight any areas to advance opportunities or foster good relations. If yes what steps will be taken?

672. How are risks graded?

2.33 Probability and Impact Assessment: Chief Investment Officer

673. Do you train all developers in the process?

674. Are there any Chief Investment Officer projects similar to this one in existence?

675. What things are likely to change?

676. What is the impact if the risk does occur?

677. Is security a central objective?

678. How realistic is the timing of introduction?

679. What is the risk appetite?

680. What action do you usually take against risks?

681. What are the levels of understanding of the future users of the outcome/results of this Chief Investment Officer project?

682. Risk urgency assessment -which of your risks could occur soon, or require a longer planning time?

683. Who should be responsible for the monitoring and tracking of the indicators youhave identified?

684. Who will be responsible for a slippage?

685. Will there be an increase in the political

conservatism?

686. Is the technology to be built new to your organization?

687. What are the current or emerging trends of culture?

688. How risk averse are you?

689. Are some people working on multiple Chief Investment Officer projects?

690. Are tool mentors available?

691. How completely has the customer been identified?

692. Is the customer willing to establish rapid communication links with the developer?

2.34 Probability and Impact Matrix: Chief Investment Officer

693. During Chief Investment Officer project executing, a team member identifies a risk that is not in the risk register. What should you do?

694. Which of your Chief Investment Officer projects should be selected when compared with other Chief Investment Officer projects?

695. What should be done NEXT?

696. Are some people working on multiple Chief Investment Officer projects?

697. Why do you need to manage Chief Investment Officer project Risk?

698. What are the methods to deal with risks?

699. Risk may be made during which step of risk management?

700. Maximize short-term return on investment?

701. Prioritized components/features?

702. What is the likelihood of a breakthrough?

703. How well is the risk understood?

704. What should be the level of difficulty in handling

the technology?

705. Are the risk data timely and relevant?

706. What needs to be DONE?

707. Do you use any methods to analyze risks?

708. Workarounds are determined during which step of risk management?

709. Are the software tools integrated with each other?

710. How are risks and risk management perceived in the Chief Investment Officer project?

2.35 Risk Data Sheet: Chief Investment Officer

711. What was measured?

712. Will revised controls lead to tolerable risk levels?

713. What are your core values?

714. What are you here for (Mission)?

715. Whom do you serve (customers)?

716. What are you trying to achieve (Objectives)?

717. Has the most cost-effective solution been chosen?

718. Are new hazards created?

719. How can it happen?

720. Potential for recurrence?

721. What is the likelihood of it happening?

722. What if client refuses?

723. How can hazards be reduced?

724. What can happen?

725. What are the main opportunities available to you

that you should grab while you can?

726. What can you do?

727. What were the Causes that contributed?

728. Type of risk identified?

2.36 Procurement Management Plan: Chief Investment Officer

729. Similar Chief Investment Officer projects?

730. Does the schedule include Chief Investment Officer project management time and change request analysis time?

731. Sensitivity analysis?

732. Are the payment terms being followed?

733. Is there a procurement management plan in place?

734. Is quality monitored from the perspective of the customers needs and expectations?

735. Is the assigned Chief Investment Officer project manager a PMP (Certified Chief Investment Officer project manager) and experienced?

736. If independent estimates will be needed as evaluation criteria, who will prepare them and when?

737. Have the key functions and capabilities been defined and assigned to each release or iteration?

738. Have process improvement efforts been completed before requirements efforts begin?

739. Have all unresolved risks been documented?

740. Are metrics used to evaluate and manage Vendors?

741. Are tasks tracked by hours?

742. Are meeting minutes captured and sent out after meetings?

743. Has the Chief Investment Officer project manager been identified?

744. Have lessons learned been conducted after each Chief Investment Officer project release?

745. Has a structured approach been used to break work effort into manageable components (WBS)?

2.37 Source Selection Criteria: Chief Investment Officer

746. Have all evaluators been trained?

747. Do you ensure you evaluate what you asked for, not what you want to see or expect to see?

748. What should preproposal conferences accomplish?

749. When should debriefings be held and how should they be scheduled?

750. When must you conduct a debriefing?

751. Is the contracting office likely to receive more purchase requests for this item or service during the coming year?

752. What aspects should the contracting officer brief the Chief Investment Officer project on prior to evaluation of proposals?

753. When is it appropriate to issue a Draft Request for Proposal (DRFP)?

754. Can you make a cost/technical tradeoff?

755. What can not be disclosed?

756. Are there any common areas of weaknesses or deficiencies in the proposals in the competitive

range?

757. Is a letter of commitment from each proposed team member and key subcontractor included?

758. What documentation is needed for a tradeoff decision?

759. What are the guiding principles for developing an evaluation report?

760. What management structure does your organization consider as optimal for performing the contract?

761. How do you manage procurement?

762. How should the oral presentations be handled?

763. What should clarifications include?

764. Why promote competition?

765. What does an evaluation address and what does a sample resemble?

2.38 Stakeholder Management Plan: Chief Investment Officer

766. How are you doing/what can be done better?

767. Are all resource assumptions documented?

768. Is the assigned Chief Investment Officer project manager a PMP (Certified Chief Investment Officer project manager) and experienced?

769. Is the Chief Investment Officer project sponsor clearly communicating the business case or rationale for why this Chief Investment Officer project is needed?

770. Does the business case include how the Chief Investment Officer project aligns with your organizations strategic goals & objectives?

771. Is there general agreement & acceptance of the current status and progress of the Chief Investment Officer project?

772. Is there an issues management plan in place?

773. Is an industry recognized mechanized support tool(s) being used for Chief Investment Officer project scheduling & tracking?

774. What is to be the method of release?

775. Are there standards for code development?

776. Is a payment system in place with proper reviews and approvals?

777. Are the key elements of a Chief Investment Officer project Charter present?

778. Have key stakeholders been identified?

779. Who would sign off on the charter?

2.39 Change Management Plan: Chief Investment Officer

780. Who will do the training?

781. Has the training provider been established?

782. What would be an estimate of the total cost for the activities required to carry out the change initiative?

783. Which relationships will change?

784. Is there a need for new relationships to be built?

785. How does the principle of senders and receivers make the Chief Investment Officer project communications effort more complex?

786. How will the stakeholders share information and transfer knowledge?

787. What is going to be done differently?

788. Impact of systems implementation on organization change?

789. How do you know the requirements you documented are the right ones?

790. What risks may occur upfront, during implementation and after implementation?

791. What is the most cynical response it can receive?

792. What new behaviours are required?

793. Do you need a new organizational structure?

794. How far reaching in your organization is the change?

795. What type of materials/channels will be available to leverage?

796. Will the readiness criteria be met prior to the training roll out?

797. How will you deal with anger about the restricting of communications due to confidentiality considerations?

798. Will the culture embrace or reject this change?

799. What processes are in place to manage knowledge about the Chief Investment Officer project?

3.0 Executing Process Group: Chief Investment Officer

800. Do Chief Investment Officer project managers understand your organizational context for Chief Investment Officer projects?

801. Were sponsors and decision makers available when needed outside regularly scheduled meetings?

802. How can your organization use a weighted decision matrix to evaluate proposals as part of source selection?

803. What is the difference between conceptual, application, and evaluative questions?

804. What are the critical steps involved in selecting measures and initiatives?

805. What are the main parts of the scope statement?

806. Do the products created live up to the necessary quality?

807. What are crucial elements of successful Chief Investment Officer project plan execution?

808. Could a new application negatively affect the current IT infrastructure?

809. Does software appear easy to learn?

810. When is the appropriate time to bring the scorecard to Board meetings?

811. Who are the Chief Investment Officer project stakeholders?

812. How is Chief Investment Officer project performance information created and distributed?

813. Just how important is your work to the overall success of the Chief Investment Officer project?

814. What is the product of your Chief Investment Officer project?

815. Will outside resources be needed to help?

816. Is activity definition the first process involved in Chief Investment Officer project time management?

817. Who will be the main sponsor?

818. How does Chief Investment Officer project management relate to other disciplines?

819. What does it mean to take a systems view of a Chief Investment Officer project?

3.1 Team Member Status Report: Chief Investment Officer

820. Why is it to be done?

821. When a teams productivity and success depend on collaboration and the efficient flow of information, what generally fails them?

822. Is there evidence that staff is taking a more professional approach toward management of your organizations Chief Investment Officer projects?

823. What specific interest groups do you have in place?

824. How does this product, good, or service meet the needs of the Chief Investment Officer project and your organization as a whole?

825. What is to be done?

826. Are the attitudes of staff regarding Chief Investment Officer project work improving?

827. How will resource planning be done?

828. How much risk is involved?

829. How can you make it practical?

830. The problem with Reward & Recognition Programs is that the truly deserving people all too

often get left out. How can you make it practical?

831. Do you have an Enterprise Chief Investment Officer project Management Office (EPMO)?

832. Will the staff do training or is that done by a third party?

833. Are the products of your organizations Chief Investment Officer projects meeting customers objectives?

834. Are your organizations Chief Investment Officer projects more successful over time?

835. Does the product, good, or service already exist within your organization?

836. Does every department have to have a Chief Investment Officer project Manager on staff?

837. How it is to be done?

838. Does your organization have the means (staff, money, contract, etc.) to produce or to acquire the product, good, or service?

3.2 Change Request: Chief Investment Officer

839. When do you create a change request?

840. Will all change requests and current status be logged?

841. How does your organization control changes before and after software is released to a customer?

842. Who can suggest changes?

843. Who will perform the change?

844. When to submit a change request?

845. How are changes requested (forms, method of communication)?

846. Are change requests logged and managed?

847. Are there requirements attributes that are strongly related to the occurrence of defects and failures?

848. What type of changes does change control take into account?

849. Has the change been highlighted and documented in the CSCI?

850. What are the requirements for urgent changes?

851. Who is communicating the change?

852. What is the change request log?

853. For which areas does this operating procedure apply?

854. How many lines of code must be changed to implement the change?

855. Who is included in the change control team?

856. Has a formal technical review been conducted to assess technical correctness?

857. Will all change requests be unconditionally tracked through this process?

3.3 Change Log: Chief Investment Officer

858. Is the change request within Chief Investment Officer project scope?

859. Who initiated the change request?

860. Is the submitted change a new change or a modification of a previously approved change?

861. Will the Chief Investment Officer project fail if the change request is not executed?

862. Should a more thorough impact analysis be conducted?

863. Do the described changes impact on the integrity or security of the system?

864. How does this relate to the standards developed for specific business processes?

865. Is the change request open, closed or pending?

866. Is the change backward compatible without limitations?

867. Is this a mandatory replacement?

868. Where do changes come from?

869. How does this change affect the timeline of the

schedule?

870. Is the requested change request a result of changes in other Chief Investment Officer project(s)?

871. When was the request approved?

872. How does this change affect scope?

873. When was the request submitted?

3.4 Decision Log: Chief Investment Officer

874. Linked to original objective?

875. How does an increasing emphasis on cost containment influence the strategies and tactics used?

876. With whom was the decision shared or considered?

877. Adversarial environment. is your opponent open to a non-traditional workflow, or will it likely challenge anything you do?

878. Do strategies and tactics aimed at less than full control reduce the costs of management or simply shift the cost burden?

879. Which variables make a critical difference?

880. What was the rationale for the decision?

881. What is the average size of your matters in an applicable measurement?

882. At what point in time does loss become unacceptable?

883. How do you define success?

884. Meeting purpose; why does this team meet?

885. How do you know when you are achieving it?

886. It becomes critical to track and periodically revisit both operational effectiveness; Are you noticing all that you need to, and are you interpreting what you see effectively?

887. Does anything need to be adjusted?

888. How does provision of information, both in terms of content and presentation, influence acceptance of alternative strategies?

889. Is everything working as expected?

890. What alternatives/risks were considered?

891. How does the use a Decision Support System influence the strategies/tactics or costs?

892. Decision-making process; how will the team make decisions?

893. How consolidated and comprehensive a story can you tell by capturing currently available incident data in a central location and through a log of key decisions during an incident?

3.5 Quality Audit: Chief Investment Officer

894. Is there a risk that information provided by management may not always be reliable?

895. Is there a written corporate quality policy?

896. How are you auditing your organizations compliance with regulations?

897. How do you indicate the extent to which your personnel would be expected to contribute to the work effort?

898. How does your organization know whether they are adhering to mission and achieving objectives?

899. How does your organization know that its systems for meeting staff extracurricular learning support requirements are appropriately effective and constructive?

900. Has a written procedure been established to identify devices during all stages of receipt, reconditioning, distribution and installation so that mix-ups are prevented?

901. What are your supplier audits?

902. Are there appropriate means for intervening if necessary?

903. How does your organization know that the support for its staff is appropriately effective and constructive?

904. Are there appropriate indicators for monitoring the effectiveness and efficiency of processes?

905. How does your organization know that its system for supporting staff research capability is appropriately effective and constructive?

906. What has changed/improved as a result of the review processes?

907. How does your organization know that its system for recruiting the best staff possible are appropriately effective and constructive?

908. Is your organizations resource allocation system properly aligned with its collection of intentions?

909. How well do you think your organization engages with the outside community?

910. How does your organization know that its system for governing staff behaviour is appropriately effective and constructive?

911. Are people allowed to contribute ideas?

912. How does your organization know that its staff entrance standards are appropriately effective and constructive and being implemented consistently?

913. How does your organization know that its staff have appropriate access to a fair and effective

grievance process?

3.6 Team Directory: Chief Investment Officer

914. Who are the Team Members?

915. How do unidentified risks impact the outcome of the Chief Investment Officer project?

916. Process decisions: are there any statutory or regulatory issues relevant to the timely execution of work?

917. Days from the time the issue is identified?

918. Decisions: is the most suitable form of contract being used?

919. Process decisions: how well was task order work performed?

920. Who should receive information (all stakeholders)?

921. Where will the product be used and/or delivered or built when appropriate?

922. Contract requirements complied with?

923. Decisions: what could be done better to improve the quality of the constructed product?

924. Process decisions: do invoice amounts match accepted work in place?

925. How does the team resolve conflicts and ensure tasks are completed?

926. Where should the information be distributed?

927. Is construction on schedule?

928. How will you accomplish and manage the objectives?

929. Process decisions: are contractors adequately prosecuting the work?

930. Have you decided when to celebrate the Chief Investment Officer projects completion date?

931. How and in what format should information be presented?

3.7 Team Operating Agreement: Chief Investment Officer

932. Do you ensure that all participants know how to use the required technology?

933. What are some potential sources of conflict among team members?

934. Has the appropriate access to relevant data and analysis capability been granted?

935. How does teaming fit in with overall organizational goals and meet organizational needs?

936. Do you listen for voice tone and word choice to understand the meaning behind words?

937. What types of accommodations will be formulated and put in place for sustaining the team?

938. Are there differences in access to communication and collaboration technology based on team member location?

939. Are there more than two functional areas represented by your team?

940. To whom do you deliver your services?

941. Have you established procedures that team members can follow to work effectively together, such as a team operating agreement?

942. Do you brief absent members after they view meeting notes or listen to a recording?

943. What is culture?

944. Do team members reside in more than two countries?

945. What are the current caseload numbers in the unit?

946. Methodologies: how will key team processes be implemented, such as training, research, work deliverable production, review and approval processes, knowledge management, and meeting procedures?

947. How will you resolve conflict efficiently and respectfully?

948. Do you use a parking lot for any items that are important and outside of the agenda?

949. What is a Virtual Team?

950. Do you record meetings for the already stated unable to attend?

951. What is group supervision?

3.8 Team Performance Assessment: Chief Investment Officer

952. What structural changes have you made or are you preparing to make?

953. To what degree do the goals specify concrete team work products?

954. Delaying market entry: how long is too long?

955. How hard do you try to make a good selection?

956. To what degree do team members frequently explore the teams purpose and its implications?

957. Effects of crew composition on crew performance: Does the whole equal the sum of its parts?

958. To what degree are sub-teams possible or necessary?

959. To what degree will team members, individually and collectively, commit time to help themselves and others learn and develop skills?

960. To what degree are the goals ambitious?

961. To what degree does the team possess adequate membership to achieve its ends?

962. If you are worried about method variance before

you collect data, what sort of design elements might you include to reduce or eliminate the threat of method variance?

963. To what degree can the team ensure that all members are individually and jointly accountable for the teams purpose, goals, approach, and work-products?

964. How do you keep key people outside the group informed about its accomplishments?

965. How hard did you try to make a good selection?

966. To what degree does the teams work approach provide opportunity for members to engage in open interaction?

967. To what degree does the teams work approach provide opportunity for members to engage in fact-based problem solving?

968. To what degree will the team adopt a concrete, clearly understood, and agreed-upon approach that will result in achievement of the teams goals?

969. To what degree do all members feel responsible for all agreed-upon measures?

970. To what degree are the teams goals and objectives clear, simple, and measurable?

971. To what degree can all members engage in open and interactive considerations?

3.9 Team Member Performance Assessment: Chief Investment Officer

972. What types of learning are targeted (e.g., cognitive, affective, psychomotor, procedural)?

973. What is a significant fact or event?

974. Are there any safeguards to prevent intentional or unintentional rating errors?

975. How should adaptive assessments be implemented?

976. Does statute or regulation require the job responsibility?

977. To what degree can team members frequently and easily communicate with one another?

978. To what degree will new and supplemental skills be introduced as the need is recognized?

979. Why do performance reviews?

980. How are evaluation results utilized?

981. What qualities does a successful Team leader possess?

982. What is the Business Management Oversight Process?

983. What instructional strategies were developed/ incorporated (e.g., direct instruction, indirect instruction, experiential learning, independent study, interactive instruction)?

984. How are training activities developed from a technical perspective?

985. What are the evaluation strategies (e.g., reaction, learning, behavior, results) used. What evaluation results did you have?

986. What variables that affect team members achievement are within your control?

987. What future plans (e.g., modifications) do you have for your program?

988. Do the goals support your organizations goals?

989. What innovations (if any) are developed to realize goals?

990. What steps have you taken to improve performance?

991. Where can team members go for more detailed information on performance measurement and assessment?

3.10 Issue Log: Chief Investment Officer

992. What effort will a change need?

993. In your work, how much time is spent on stakeholder identification?

994. Is the issue log kept in a safe place?

995. Who needs to know and how much?

996. Are the stakeholders getting the information they need, are they consulted, are concerns addressed?

997. What is the status of the issue?

998. What date was the issue resolved?

999. Why multiple evaluators?

1000. What are the typical contents?

1001. Persistence; will users learn a work around or will they be bothered every time?

1002. Who is the issue assigned to?

1003. Which team member will work with each stakeholder?

1004. What is the impact on the Business Case?

4.0 Monitoring and Controlling Process Group: Chief Investment Officer

1005. Were decisions made in a timely manner?

1006. Did you implement the program as designed?

1007. In what way has the program come up with innovative measures for problem-solving?

1008. Key stakeholders to work with. How many potential communications channels exist on the Chief Investment Officer project?

1009. How do you monitor progress?

1010. Purpose: toward what end is the evaluation being conducted?

1011. What were things that you did very well and want to do the same again on the next Chief Investment Officer project?

1012. What were things that you did well, and could improve, and how?

1013. What resources (both financial and non-financial) are available/needed?

1014. What input will you be required to provide the Chief Investment Officer project team?

1015. How well did the team follow the chosen processes?

1016. If action is called for, what form should it take?

1017. Is the schedule for the set products being met?

1018. Feasibility: how much money, time, and effort can you put into this?

1019. How is agile portfolio management done?

1020. How is agile Chief Investment Officer project management done?

1021. What areas were overlooked on this Chief Investment Officer project?

4.1 Project Performance Report: Chief Investment Officer

1022. To what degree is the information network consistent with the structure of the formal organization?

1023. To what degree can team members meet frequently enough to accomplish the teams ends?

1024. To what degree will the team ensure that all members equitably share the work essential to the success of the team?

1025. To what degree does the informal organization make use of individual resources and meet individual needs?

1026. To what degree can team members vigorously define the teams purpose in considerations with others who are not part of the functioning team?

1027. To what degree are the goals realistic?

1028. To what degree are the skill areas critical to team performance present?

1029. What is the degree to which rules govern information exchange between groups?

1030. What degree are the relative importance and priority of the goals clear to all team members?

1031. To what degree do team members understand one anothers roles and skills?

1032. To what degree do team members feel that the purpose of the team is important, if not exciting?

1033. To what degree does the information network provide individuals with the information they require?

1034. How is the data used?

1035. To what degree does the funding match the requirement?

1036. To what degree will the approach capitalize on and enhance the skills of all team members in a manner that takes into consideration other demands on members of the team?

1037. To what degree are the tasks requirements reflected in the flow and storage of information?

1038. To what degree do team members articulate the teams work approach?

4.2 Variance Analysis: Chief Investment Officer

1039. Contemplated overhead expenditure for each period based on the best information currently is available?

1040. What is the incurrence of actual indirect costs in excess of budgets, by element of expense?

1041. Are your organizations and items of cost assigned to each pool identified?

1042. How do you identify potential or actual overruns and underruns?

1043. How are variances affected by multiple material and labor categories?

1044. When, during the last four quarters, did a primary business event occur causing a fluctuation?

1045. How does your organization allocate the cost of shared expenses and services?

1046. Are significant decision points, constraints, and interfaces identified as key milestones?

1047. Are there externalities from having some customers, even if they are unprofitable in the short run?

1048. Why do variances exist?

1049. Are the actual costs used for variance analysis reconcilable with data from the accounting system?

1050. Is all contract work included in the CWBS?

1051. What business event causes fluctuations?

1052. What is the performance to date and material commitment?

1053. Can process improvements lead to unfavorable variances?

1054. Are procedures for variance analysis documented and consistently applied at the control account level and selected WBS and organizational levels at least monthly as a routine task?

1055. Who are responsible for overhead performance control of related costs?

1056. Wbs elements contractually specified for reporting of status to your organization (lowest level only)?

1057. Are there changes in the overhead pool and/or organization structures?

4.3 Earned Value Status: Chief Investment Officer

1058. Are you hitting your Chief Investment Officer projects targets?

1059. Where are your problem areas?

1060. Verification is a process of ensuring that the developed system satisfies the stakeholders agreements and specifications; Are you building the product right? What do you verify?

1061. Earned value can be used in almost any Chief Investment Officer project situation and in almost any Chief Investment Officer project environment. it may be used on large Chief Investment Officer projects, medium sized Chief Investment Officer projects, tiny Chief Investment Officer projects (in cut-down form), complex and simple Chief Investment Officer projects and in any market sector. some people, of course, know all about earned value, they have used it for years - but perhaps not as effectively as they could have?

1062. Validation is a process of ensuring that the developed system will actually achieve the stakeholders desired outcomes; Are you building the right product? What do you validate?

1063. Where is evidence-based earned value in your organization reported?

1064. What is the unit of forecast value?

1065. How much is it going to cost by the finish?

1066. If earned value management (EVM) is so good in determining the true status of a Chief Investment Officer project and Chief Investment Officer project its completion, why is it that hardly any one uses it in information systems related Chief Investment Officer projects?

1067. How does this compare with other Chief Investment Officer projects?

1068. When is it going to finish?

4.4 Risk Audit: Chief Investment Officer

1069. Are all financial transactions accurately recorded (receipted, banked)?

1070. Do you record and file all audits?

1071. What are the differences and similarities between strategic and operational risks in your organization?

1072. Auditor independence: a burdensome constraint or a core value?

1073. Does your organization communicate regularly and effectively with its members?

1074. What are the strategic implications with clients when auditors focus audit resources based on business-level risks?

1075. What does your data tell you about your risks?

1076. Are testing tools available and suitable?

1077. Are team members trained in the use of the tools?

1078. Are corresponding safety and risk management policies posted for all to see?

1079. Who audits the auditor?

1080. Do your financial policies and procedures ensure that each step in financial handling (receipt, recording, banking, reporting) is not completed by one person?

1081. Is risk an management agenda item?

1082. Is there a screening process that will ensure all participants have the fitness and skills required to safely participate?

1083. Is Chief Investment Officer project scope stable?

1084. How are risk appetites expressed?

1085. Does the Chief Investment Officer project team have experience with the technology to be implemented?

1086. Do all coaches/instructors/leaders have appropriate and current accreditation?

1087. Have top software and customer managers formally committed to support the Chief Investment Officer project?

4.5 Contractor Status Report: Chief Investment Officer

1088. What was the overall budget or estimated cost?

1089. If applicable; describe your standard schedule for new software version releases. Are new software version releases included in the standard maintenance plan?

1090. What was the final actual cost?

1091. How is risk transferred?

1092. What process manages the contracts?

1093. Who can list a Chief Investment Officer project as organization experience, your organization or a previous employee of your organization?

1094. What was the actual budget or estimated cost for your organizations services?

1095. How long have you been using the services?

1096. What was the budget or estimated cost for your organizations services?

1097. Are there contractual transfer concerns?

1098. Describe how often regular updates are made to the proposed solution. Are corresponding regular updates included in the standard maintenance plan?

1099. What are the minimum and optimal bandwidth requirements for the proposed solution?

1100. How does the proposed individual meet each requirement?

1101. What is the average response time for answering a support call?

4.6 Formal Acceptance: Chief Investment Officer

1102. Did the Chief Investment Officer project achieve its MOV?

1103. Who supplies data?

1104. What function(s) does it fill or meet?

1105. Who would use it?

1106. Have all comments been addressed?

1107. What features, practices, and processes proved to be strengths or weaknesses?

1108. Do you buy-in installation services?

1109. Was the Chief Investment Officer project work done on time, within budget, and according to specification?

1110. Do you perform formal acceptance or burn-in tests?

1111. Was the Chief Investment Officer project goal achieved?

1112. Is formal acceptance of the Chief Investment Officer project product documented and distributed?

1113. What was done right?

1114. Was business value realized?

1115. What are the requirements against which to test, Who will execute?

1116. Did the Chief Investment Officer project manager and team act in a professional and ethical manner?

1117. How does your team plan to obtain formal acceptance on your Chief Investment Officer project?

1118. Was the Chief Investment Officer project managed well?

1119. Was the client satisfied with the Chief Investment Officer project results?

1120. Does it do what client said it would?

1121. Was the sponsor/customer satisfied?

5.0 Closing Process Group: Chief Investment Officer

1122. Did the delivered product meet the specified requirements and goals of the Chief Investment Officer project?

1123. What were things that you did very well and want to do the same again on the next Chief Investment Officer project?

1124. What is the overall risk of the Chief Investment Officer project to your organization?

1125. Will the Chief Investment Officer project deliverable(s) replace a current asset or group of assets?

1126. What areas were overlooked on this Chief Investment Officer project?

1127. When will the Chief Investment Officer project be done?

1128. What areas were overlooked on this Chief Investment Officer project?

1129. How will staff learn how to use the deliverables?

1130. Is there a clear cause and effect between the activity and the lesson learned?

1131. What is the Chief Investment Officer project

Management Process?

1132. Did the Chief Investment Officer project team have enough people to execute the Chief Investment Officer project plan?

1133. What do you need to do?

1134. Did you do what you said you were going to do?

1135. What level of risk does the proposed budget represent to the Chief Investment Officer project?

1136. Can the lesson learned be replicated?

1137. Is this a follow-on to a previous Chief Investment Officer project?

1138. How will you do it?

5.1 Procurement Audit: Chief Investment Officer

1139. Is the functioning of automatic disbursement programs tested by an independent party?

1140. Was a sufficient competitive environment created?

1141. Are known obligations, such as salaries and contracts, encumbered at the beginning of the year?

1142. When performance conditions were detailed in the tender documentation, did the contracting authority verify if the tenders received met the already stated requirements?

1143. Does your organization make sources of information beyond the tender documents equally available for all the candidates?

1144. Are buyers rotated so that they do not deal with the same vendors year in and year out?

1145. Has your organization taken a well-grounded decision about the procurement procedure chosen and has it documented the process?

1146. Are checks used in numeric sequence?

1147. Are the purchase order forms designed for efficient and simple completion?

1148. Does your organization maintain a current file of vendors and vendor catalogues?

1149. Is the weighting set coherent, convincing and leaving little scope for arbitrary and random evaluation and ranking?

1150. Does each policy statement contain the legal reference(s) on which the policy is based?

1151. Are the rules for automatic payment in computer programs approved by management prior to implementation?

1152. Were calculations used in evaluation adequate and correct?

1153. How do you avoid delays at any stage/ stages of the procurement process?

1154. Are all initial purchase contracts made by the purchasing organization?

1155. Are idle funds invested, and is interest distributed to the various activity accounts at least annually?

1156. Was the dynamic purchasing system set up following the rules of open procedure?

1157. Was the suitability of candidates accurately assessed?

1158. Are procurement policies and practices in line with (international) good practice standards?

5.2 Contract Close-Out: Chief Investment Officer

1159. Parties: Authorized?

1160. Have all contracts been completed?

1161. Change in circumstances?

1162. Was the contract complete without requiring numerous changes and revisions?

1163. Was the contract sufficiently clear so as not to result in numerous disputes and misunderstandings?

1164. Change in knowledge?

1165. How does it work?

1166. How/when used ?

1167. What is capture management?

1168. Have all contract records been included in the Chief Investment Officer project archives?

1169. Change in attitude or behavior?

1170. Has each contract been audited to verify acceptance and delivery?

1171. How is the contracting office notified of the automatic contract close-out?

1172. What happens to the recipient of services?

1173. Are the signers the authorized officials?

1174. Parties: who is involved?

1175. Why Outsource?

1176. Have all contracts been closed?

1177. Was the contract type appropriate?

1178. Have all acceptance criteria been met prior to final payment to contractors?

5.3 Project or Phase Close-Out: Chief Investment Officer

1179. Which changes might a stakeholder be required to make as a result of the Chief Investment Officer project?

1180. What information did each stakeholder need to contribute to the Chief Investment Officer projects success?

1181. Planned completion date?

1182. What are the mandatory communication needs for each stakeholder?

1183. Does the lesson describe a function that would be done differently the next time?

1184. Who controlled the resources for the Chief Investment Officer project?

1185. What information is each stakeholder group interested in?

1186. What security considerations needed to be addressed during the procurement life cycle?

1187. Planned remaining costs?

1188. What could have been improved?

1189. What stakeholder group needs, expectations,

and interests are being met by the Chief Investment Officer project?

1190. Is the lesson significant, valid, and applicable?

1191. What advantages do the an individual interview have over a group meeting, and vice-versa?

1192. Complete yes or no?

1193. What is a Risk?

1194. What was the preferred delivery mechanism?

1195. What are the informational communication needs for each stakeholder?

1196. What is this stakeholder expecting?

5.4 Lessons Learned: Chief Investment Officer

1197. Overall, how effective were the efforts to prepare you and your organization for the impact of the product/service of the Chief Investment Officer project?

1198. How clear were you on your role in the Chief Investment Officer project?

1199. What is the expected lifespan of the deliverable?

1200. How well did the scope of the Chief Investment Officer project match what was defined in the Chief Investment Officer project Proposal?

1201. What were the success factors?

1202. How do individuals resolve conflict?

1203. To what extent was the evolution of risks communicated?

1204. How effective were the communications materials in providing and orienting team members about the details of the Chief Investment Officer project?

1205. What were the desired outcomes?

1206. What is the quality and content of communication?

1207. What worked well or did not work well, either for this Chief Investment Officer project or for the Chief Investment Officer project team?

1208. What skills are required for the task?

1209. Was there a Chief Investment Officer project Definition document. Was there a Chief Investment Officer project Plan. Were they used during the Chief Investment Officer project?

1210. How smooth do you feel Integration has been?

1211. What were the main bottlenecks on the process?

1212. What report generation capability is needed?

1213. If issue escalation was required, how effectively were issues resolved?

1214. Are you in full regulatory compliance?

1215. What were the challenges and pitfalls?

Index

assessing   89, 95
Assessment   5-6, 8-9, 19, 143, 197-198, 206, 237, 239-240
assets   43, 256
assigned   141, 149, 155, 162, 194, 197, 212, 216, 241, 246
assigning   170
assignment   4, 163, 193-194
assist   8, 65, 84, 103, 184, 193
assistant   7
associated   146, 155, 202
Assume   204-205
Assumption   3, 151
assurance   17, 141, 149, 158-159, 198
attached   174
attainable   34, 196
attempted   37
attempting   101
attend 23, 236
attendance   40
attendant   87
attended   40
attention   11, 110
attitude   260
attitudes   222
attribute   187
attributes   3, 107, 145-146, 162, 224
audiences   188
audited   260
auditing   17, 96, 126, 230
auditor 250
auditors   250
audits   230, 250
author 1
authority   70, 131, 143-144, 196, 200, 258
authorized   142, 156, 260-261
automatic   258-260
available   20, 24, 38, 49, 61, 64, 78, 103, 120, 155, 160, 162,
177, 205, 207, 210, 219-220, 229, 242, 246, 250, 258
Average   11, 25, 42, 57, 73, 91, 103, 128, 174, 228, 253
averse 207
avoided   202
background   9
backing   164
backup   150

controlled 59, 262
controls 21, 61, 66, 80, 84, 86, 93, 97, 99-100, 102, 166, 204, 210
convention 111
conversion 151
convey 1
convincing 259
cooperate 183
Copyright 1
corporate 230
correct 43, 92, 139, 141, 158, 177, 259
corrective 101, 204
correspond 8-9
costing 48
counter 135
counting 106, 144
countries 236
counts 106
course 29, 53, 248
covering 8, 97
coworker 112
craziest 113
create 25, 63, 117, 124, 126, 189, 224
created 68, 96, 130, 134, 159, 205, 210, 220-221, 258
creating 7, 50, 137, 149, 188
creative 19
creativity 86
credible 183
crisis 25
criteria 2, 5, 8-9, 34, 37, 40, 67, 78, 84, 88, 95, 122, 129, 135, 147, 150, 183, 212, 214, 219, 261
CRITERION 2, 15, 27, 43, 58, 75, 92, 104
critical 34, 39-40, 68, 81, 96, 100, 114, 151, 165, 220, 228-229, 244
cross-sell 123
crucial 71, 164, 173, 220
crystal 10
culture 31, 66, 190, 195-196, 207, 219, 236
current 29, 43, 55, 57, 62-64, 78, 94, 106, 116, 122-123, 151-152, 156, 180, 192, 195, 198, 207, 216, 220, 224, 236, 251, 256, 259
currently 36, 126, 155, 229, 246
custom 25
customer 20, 28-29, 38-39, 89, 97, 102, 110, 112, 116, 145-146, 181, 187, 202-203, 207, 224, 251, 255

logged 224
logical 169
logically   159
longer 100, 206
long-term   94, 110-111
losing 47
losses 24, 27
lowest 247
magnitude   85
maintain   92, 111, 126, 259
maintained   87, 156, 158
makers 84, 94, 220
making   22, 63, 76, 85, 120, 192, 196
manage   30, 36, 52, 56-57, 59-60, 78, 86, 88-89, 115, 118, 132, 139, 147-148, 176, 191, 194, 200, 205, 208, 213, 215, 219, 234
manageable   41, 213
managed   7, 38, 62, 66, 70, 78-79, 82-83, 95, 98, 150, 224, 255
management 1, 3-5, 8-9, 20, 23-24, 33, 42, 46, 70-73, 82-83, 85-86, 88, 90, 114-115, 123, 130, 137, 139, 141, 143, 149-151, 157-159, 171-173, 177-179, 181-182, 187-188, 192, 195, 197-198, 200, 202-203, 208-209, 212, 215-216, 218, 221-223, 228, 230, 236, 239, 243, 249-251, 257, 259-260
manager   7, 9, 20, 30, 38, 125, 132, 149, 158, 197, 212-213, 216, 223, 255
managers   2, 129, 131, 180, 220, 251
manages   83, 252
managing   2, 129, 131, 134-135, 143
mandate   132
mandatory   226, 262
manner   24, 87, 155, 180, 194, 242, 245, 255
mantle 117
Mapping   66-67, 70
margin 159
market 164, 237, 248
marketer   7
Marketing   125
markets   16
Maslow   172
material   156-157, 188, 246-247
materials   1, 219, 264
matrices   147
Matrix 2-5, 135, 147, 193-194, 208, 220

matter 37, 53, 55
matters   228
Maximize   208
maximizing   117
maximum   131
McClellan   172
McGregor   172
meaning   235
meaningful   45, 108
measurable   28, 34, 130, 238
measure   2, 9, 17, 21, 34, 37, 43, 48-50, 52-53, 56-57, 59, 65,
75, 77, 82, 88, 90, 96, 101-102, 133, 135-136, 183, 187, 191
measured   22, 45, 47-48, 56-57, 82, 96, 99, 194, 210
measures   44-46, 49, 55, 57, 62-65, 78, 94, 96, 98, 137, 192,
204, 220, 238, 242
measuring   92
mechanical   1
mechanism   263
mechanisms   192
mechanized   216
medium   248
meeting   31, 33, 97, 179, 185, 192, 195, 200, 213, 223, 228,
230, 236, 263
meetings   29, 40, 144, 149, 158, 213, 220-221, 236
megatrends   107
member   5-6, 38, 105, 208, 215, 222, 235, 239, 241
members   41-42, 67, 103, 150, 158, 173, 177, 198, 233, 235-
240, 244-245, 250, 264
membership   237
mentors   207
method   44, 163, 189, 216, 224, 237-238
methods   28, 40, 54, 59, 183, 198, 208-209
metrics 4, 33, 63, 101, 189-190, 197, 213
milestone   3, 133, 141, 158, 164, 166
milestones   33, 134, 162, 179, 246
minimize   130
minimizing   66, 117
minimum   253
minority   20
minutes   31, 81, 179, 213
missed 48, 126
missing 63, 106, 162, 186
mission 70, 116, 210, 230

number   25, 42, 49, 57, 73, 91, 103, 128, 170, 266
numbers   110, 236
numeric   258
numerous   260
objection   16, 24
objective   7, 49, 136, 181, 193, 206, 228
objectives   18, 20-21, 27, 33, 39, 70, 95, 101, 106, 121-123,
145, 172, 180, 210, 216, 223, 230, 234, 238
observe   196
observed   83
obsolete   107
obstacles   17, 184
obtain 125, 255
obtained   38, 151
obtaining   55
obviously   10
occurrence   224
occurring   90, 205
occurs 25, 93, 130-131
offerings   64, 81
office   187, 214, 223, 260
Officer 1-6, 8-13, 16-26, 28-57, 59, 61-135, 137-139, 141-145, 147,
149-153, 155-156, 158-162, 164-166, 168, 170-187, 189, 191, 193,
195, 197-210, 212-214, 216-224, 226-228, 230, 233-235, 237, 239,
241-244, 246, 248-252, 254-258, 260, 262-265
officials261
offshore   145
onboarding   198
one-time   7
ongoing   90, 99, 161, 175
opened   193
operates   121
operating   5, 52-53, 100, 225, 235
operation   102, 174
operations   9, 92, 100-101, 185
operators   96
opponent   228
opposite   116, 121
opposition   110
optimal   87, 90, 215, 253
optimize   85, 92
optimized   115
optimiztic   173

process   1-7, 9, 27, 29, 32, 34-35, 39, 55, 58-66, 68-73, 80,
83, 94-95, 97-98, 100, 102-103, 130, 137, 140-141, 143, 146-147,
149-152, 168, 172, 187, 191, 196, 198, 206, 212, 220-221, 225, 229,
232-234, 239, 242, 247-248, 251-252, 256-259, 265
processes   48, 57, 59, 61, 63-65, 67-68, 70-71, 73, 101, 130-
131, 138, 152, 179, 192, 219, 226, 231, 236, 243, 254
produce   70, 131, 168, 223
produced   70, 137, 150
produces   163
producing   147, 150
product   1, 54, 63-64, 124-125, 138, 142, 164, 185, 189, 202,
221-223, 233, 248, 254, 256, 264
production   29, 90, 109, 130, 236
productive   193
products   1, 18, 20, 50, 116, 127, 133, 147, 186, 220, 223,
237, 243
profit   190
profits   186
program   25, 51, 101, 130, 204, 240, 242
programme   137
programs   222, 258-259
progress   42, 56, 88, 100, 120, 133, 183, 192, 216, 242
project 2-4, 6-8, 22, 25, 33, 49, 59, 66-67, 90, 95, 102, 105, 107,
114-115, 117, 119, 121, 123, 125, 129-135, 137-139, 141-145, 147,
149-153, 158-162, 164-166, 170-187, 189, 193, 195, 197-206, 208-
209, 212-214, 216-223, 226-227, 233, 242-244, 248-249, 251-252,
254-257, 260, 262-265
projected   155-156
projects   2, 46, 114, 123, 129-130, 138, 147, 149-150, 153,
173, 176, 180, 206-208, 212, 220, 222-223, 234, 248-249, 262
promising   124
promote   50, 172, 215
promotion   195
promptly   182
proofing   83
proper 93, 143, 217
properly   30, 32, 194, 231
Proposal   164, 214, 264
proposals   94, 214, 220
proposed   22, 47, 54, 77, 87, 142, 145, 215, 252-253, 257
protect   66, 117, 139
protection   117
protocols   189

proved 254
provide   25, 64, 114, 121, 134-135, 145, 157, 173, 176, 184,
189, 238, 242, 245
provided   11, 95, 141, 158, 172, 180, 230
provider   218
providers   85, 135
providing   93, 132, 134, 164, 176, 264
provision   198, 229
publisher   1
pulled 114
purchase   7, 214, 258-259
purchased   156
purchasing   259
purpose   2, 9, 116, 170, 183, 228, 237-238, 242, 244-245
purposes   142
qualified   41, 61, 67, 71-73, 149
qualifies   61, 66
qualify 68, 71
qualities   239
quality 1, 4-5, 9, 17, 47, 49, 54, 60, 70-71, 90, 96, 99, 121, 141,
149-150, 158-159, 176, 179, 187-192, 195, 198, 212, 220, 230, 233,
264
quantified   99
quarters   246
question   10, 15, 27, 43, 58, 75, 92, 104, 106, 202
questions   7-8, 10, 175, 220
quickly 9, 59-60, 67, 203
radically   63
raised 180
random   259
ranking 259
rather 53, 108
rating 239
rational   155
rationale   197, 216, 228
reached   21
reaching   123, 173, 219
reaction   240
reactivate   122
readiness   29, 197, 219
readings   93
realistic   21, 69, 117, 139, 159, 206, 244
reality 185, 203

Printed in Great Britain
by Amazon

18518404R00178